A View From The Floor

A
View
From The Floor

The Journal of
a U.S. Senate Page Boy

Frank Madison

Prentice-Hall, Inc., Englewood Cliffs, New Jersey

A VIEW FROM THE FLOOR: The Journal of a U.S. Senate Page Boy
by Frank Madison
© 1967 by Prentice-Hall, Inc.
Copyright under International and Pan American
Copyright Conventions
Library of Congress Catalog Card Number: 67–24025
Printed in the United States of America
T 94186
Prentice-Hall International, Inc., London
Prentice-Hall of Australia, Pty. Ltd., Sydney
Prentice-Hall of Canada, Ltd., Toronto
Prentice-Hall of India Private Ltd., New Delhi
Prentice-Hall of Japan, Inc., Tokyo

To

My Parents

Who Advised

and

Earle Clements

Who Consented

Introduction   9

The Diary   23

Biographical Notes   155

A View From The Floor

Introduction

Eleven years ago I served during one Congressional session as a Senate page boy. For seven months I worked close to John F. Kennedy, Lyndon B. Johnson and Bobby Baker, among others, and had a marvelous time doing it. Recently I read over the journal I kept during those months. I then showed the journal to several friends, who pronounced it a "historic" document and suggested that it should be published, arguing that many people would enjoy reading what a sixteen-year-old boy had to say about famous men, many of whom are more famous now than they were ten years ago. The Senate of the 1950s was the training ground for the nation's leaders during the 1960s, they pointed out, and a document of that period has greater interest today than when it was written. The "page's view" of the Senate has, moreover, never been expressed.

I arrived in Washington early in January 1956, shortly after my sixteenth birthday. My appointment was a patronage position, arranged for me by Senator Earle C. Clements of Kentucky, the Assistant Majority Leader of the Senate, and I was known to the staff of the Senate as "Clements' page." Officially, however, I was an employee of the Senate, working under the supervision of the staff of the Secretary of the Senate. Senator Clements, as my sponsor, took an interest in my general welfare and delighted in introducing me to all sorts of people. I was also chosen, when available, to run errands requested by Clements or his staff, and if the Senate adjourned early I might spend a few hours in the Senator's office helping with the mail or performing other tasks.

The organization of the pages, like that of the Senate itself, followed party lines. Below the Secretary of the Senate, who, though appointed by the majority party, served the entire Senate, were the Secretaries for the Majority and Minority who supervised the activities of the staffs serving the two parties. The pages were divided into two sections, Republican and Democratic, with headquarters in the cloakrooms of the two parties at opposite ends of the Senate floor. The Majority and Minority Secretaries had desks on the floor itself and separate offices nearby. They were actually always on the move while the Senate was in session, conferring, giving orders to pages, contacting senators and making sure that the scheduled business of the day proceeded as planned. The Secretaries had a number of assistants, who were stationed at the switchboards in the cloakrooms and whose job was to receive and relay messages. Next were the pages themselves, whose station was the cloakroom or the steps of the Senate rostrum but who were also almost perpetually in motion. The pages delivered messages to senators on the floor, as instructed by the switchboard operators, or ran errands that might take them all over the Capitol area or even to distant parts of the city. The pages seated on the rostrum facing the Senate floor were expected to respond to the requests of senators.

One was thus either a Democratic or a Republican page and shared to some degree in the larger rivalry of the two parties. If a page owed his appointment to a Democratic senator, he naturally wished to work on the Democratic side and was reluctant to run errands for Republicans. A certain amount of shifting back and forth was necessary, however. When one side of the rostrum was particularly busy, its depleted ranks might be temporarily supplemented by pages borrowed from the other. More important was the fact that the majority party controlled much more than a majority of the patronage. There were more Democratic senators to run errands for, and the majority party had the responsibility of managing the business of the Senate; even so it was necessary for some Democratic pages to work on the Republican side. The expedient of rotating Democratic pages was adopted, requiring new arrivals to serve an apprenticeship on the Republican side. I thus worked as a Republican page for a number of weeks before returning to the Democratic side for the remainder of the session.

There is a common impression that every senator has a page. Actually the page corps in the Senate numbered between 25 and 30, and working strength at any given time during a session was usually eight or ten on a side. The pages' internal organization reflected not only the Senate's party division but also its seniority system. Each side had its Head Page, chosen strictly on the basis of years of service (rather than chronological age). The Head Page was normally a fourth-year boy who had spent his entire high-school career at the Capitol Page School while working in the Senate. Head pages did not customarily run errands themselves. They remained seated at the back of the rostrum, monitoring the buzzer system by which pages were summoned from the cloakrooms, making certain that a sufficient number of pages was always available on the floor and generally ensuring decorum and relative silence.

Senate pages normally attended the Capitol Page School, joining the fifty pages from the House of Representatives and the handful from the Supreme Court in classes from 6:30 A.M. to 10:30 A.M. before reporting for work at 11:00 A.M. to prepare for the sessions, which began at noon. I was fortunately free of this obligation because I had completed high school before I came to the Senate. I had decided to take a year off between high school and college, and freedom from the routine of studies enabled me to concentrate much more fully on what I could learn at work. Pages with homework to do were naturally eager to be excused from work as soon as possible, but I was quite happy to stay around in the hope of observing something of interest. Most pages were sent home at the end of the normal working day, only a few

11

staying on the floor during late evening sessions. I liked to work during those sessions because the senators became more casual and conversational. With their offices closed for the day, they would spend the idle hours chatting informally in the cloakrooms and corridors.

As pages we had a very special position in the legislative process. There were some privileges that pages shared only with senators. Only pages and senators could enter the sanctuary of the Senate Marble Room; other senatorial assistants were excluded. The Senate floor was the major sphere of activity only for senators, a few clerks and pages; others were permitted here only when performing special missions. Our privileges, of course, resulted from the fact that pages matched in unimportance the importance of senators. Only pages were sufficiently unimportant to be permitted into the Marble Room, where senators retreated for complete privacy and immunity from constituents and staff. The pages didn't matter; they could be ignored. They served useful purposes by running errands and were too young to embarrass senators by their presence.

Such inconsequence meant that a page had an unusual vantage point from which to observe what was going on. The page's position was also special in that the function he performed had some real importance. Pages had to be available at all times, for it was difficult to predict when critical votes would be called. On such occasions pages became a tensely disciplined army with a vital task—to get senators to the floor in time to vote. Constant preparations were necessary for these sudden crises. The staff had to remain always informed of the whereabouts of senators of its party, where they could be reached at any time. When the vote was called, scarcely ten minutes were available in which to produce the senators. Pages manned all the cloakroom telephones and raced down back corridors to secret offices—small rooms in remote corners of the Capitol where the few senators fortunate enough to possess them hid themselves away from interruptions less urgent than the summonses we brought—carrying out the orders of the Secretaries for the Majority and Minority. At such times pages were frantically busy and desperately needed adjuncts to the legislative process.

A number of senators use their patronage as an award for merit, offering page positions to high-school students from their states on the basis of some standard of accomplishment. Other senators treat their patronage as a form of charitable assistance, offering page positions to orphans or boys with widowed mothers to support. Some senators lose track of their patronage, and it is often handled by members of their staffs. The caliber of individual pages is as varied as is the method of selection.

Senator Clements, "my" senator, was the only member of the Senate with two pages—a testament to the power of an assistant majority leader. His senior page, who had served in the Senate for several terms, was an orphan, whom the Senator treated very much as an adopted son. In my case, becoming a page was my own idea; Senator Clements was, I suspect, intrigued by my insistence and generously arranged for my appointment as his second page. As my journal reveals, he continued to participate actively in my education during my time in the Senate by introducing me to all variety of people with unflagging enthusiasm.

Yet Senator Clements, for all his kindness, remained a relatively remote figure. By far the most salient of my many bosses was Bobby Baker. Baker occupied a unique position in the Senate, only partially because of his formal powers as Secretary for the Majority. His official responsibility was to see that the business of the Senate was accomplished, that the bills scheduled for passage actually did pass and that senators who wanted to deliver speeches had the chance to do so. He was the man who turned decisions into results. As such, he controlled the lives and actions of the pages directly, just as he kept track of the lives and actions of senators more discreetly and indirectly. The position he held was an important one, which he transformed by talent and ingenuity into a crucial one. He possessed the tact to give orders to senators over whom he had no coercive authority, as well as an infinite knowledge of the subtleties of Capitol organization stemming from long years in the inner circle. He had literally "grown up" in the Senate, having begun as a page himself. Bobby Baker was the linchpin in the system, the link between the policy organs and the machinery of implementation.

Baker's authority and personality were awesome to me as a

13

page, and his career was a success story that I might have been inspired to emulate. He too had been a page and at the age of twenty-seven had ascended to the height of the Senate's organizational hierarchy. He was serenely self-assured and deft in his personal dealings, amazingly cool and skillful in his management of the famous and difficult men in his charge. He may not have been included in the innermost councils where policy decisions were made, but superficially he seemed to be the one man who really ran the Senate. He knew what was to happen each day, and he made it happen. He was the man senators asked for permission if they wished to leave the chamber for a day or the city for a weekend; he alone could tell them whether or not their votes would be necessary on a pending issue. As senators streamed onto the floor from offices or hearings, Bobby Baker told them how to vote. He told them what the party position on the particular issue was and also whether or not it would be more consistent with their own past records to vote against their party in this instance. (It was a strange procedure to behold: "Senator Morse, you're supposed to vote yes. Senator Byrd, you should probably vote no on this one.")

Freshman senators might receive their instructions from pages, but most senior senators expected to receive their orders directly from Bobby Baker. He possessed the private telephone numbers of senators; he knew the locations of their secret offices and where they were most likely to be at any given moment. It was he who dispatched the pages to bring senators back to the floor in time to vote. He also played a significant role in determining the outcome of decisions by his preliminary canvasses. By ascertaining the likely results of votes on important issues, he managed to influence decisions concerning whether or not to bring matters to the floor for formal votes. His field was reality. The thorough command he possessed of this particular world gave him considerable influence over all proposals.

I knew nothing of the wide-ranging business activities that ultimately made Bobby Baker a notorious figure and lost him his job in the Senate. I believe in fact that most of his business ventures had not been initiated at the time I knew him. His subsequent

14

career, however, does not seem altogether incomprehensible in terms of my recollections of him in 1956. The awe with which he inspired me when I was sixteen is clear from my journal; but it was partially his suave worldliness that so impressed me, that make him seem, in retrospect at least, to have been potentially "capable" of piecing together an intricate business empire. My admiration for him was founded upon amazement that he had risen so far so fast. I felt confident that more would be heard of him in the future. I thought he would ultimately go into politics and perhaps run for the governorship of his native South Carolina; I was certain that he had talent and ambition. At the time I was describing him in my journal, he was not known publicly, and I made a point of delineating the important role he was performing at the center of national affairs. He was my personal boss and potentially my model and mentor.

Although the position Bobby Baker occupied in my world as a page is clear from the journal, the one occupied by Lyndon Johnson is possibly less clear. Johnson was already then a national figure most of whose actions were too well covered to require any additional notice from me. His dominance over the Senate was, besides, so constant and overwhelming that one tended to take it for granted and to single out for comment the special triumphs of others while ignoring the indefatigible efforts of the master parliamentarian. Johnson was always present, speaking on the floor many times during almost any day and handling procedural matters in terse and businesslike fashion. At other times he would sprawl in a chair on the floor or in the cloakroom, making telephone calls in endless succession. He covered the expanses of the Capitol with a sweeping stride, restless, tall, always immaculately groomed. There was an authority in his gait, his long arms and sudden commanding voice that made pages scurry out of his way with greater rapidity than with any other person and carry out his instructions with desperate anxiety.

It is interesting to read my "prediction" that Johnson would never be President, not because the prediction was wrong, but rather because the analysis on which it was based still seems quite defensible. My contention was that Johnson was not photogenic,

15

that the image that filtered through the mass media seemed an odd distortion of the man I observed every day. The much greater exposure that he has received since his unexpected succession to the Presidency could be said to have actually reinforced the validity of my original observation. His features fit awkwardly into a photograph, as does his voice between the elegantly modulated syllables of a television commentator. Lyndon Johnson in person in the Senate was very different. He seemed handsome because of his height, his careful dress, his ease of movement. His accent was not out of place in a chamber where Southern voices seemed to predominate. He was capable of terrifying many people more important than pages when his temper was aroused. But he also possessed a grace and even a delicacy in his personal dealings that were incongruous with his public image and that failed to come through effectively in his formal speeches.

Johnson controlled the Senate with a tight rein but only because he worked hard to merit the Senate's trust. A majority leader has little automatic power over his colleagues, each of whom has an independent base of power. Johnson earned his power by hard work, by faithfully doing what the Senate wanted done but would have found difficult to accomplish without him. As far as I was able to observe, Johnson seemed essentially an honest broker, a manager who insisted only that things be done; he did not insist that they always be done in his way. I can remember once his shouting to the chairman of an important committee: "I don't care what's in your bill. Just get it out here."

Johnson cast himself in the role of master of everything and servant of everyone. He tried to give each senator as much power as he seemed to deserve in terms of the Senate's own standards. My recollection is that during the entire session he spoke out at length on a substantive issue only once—on the natural-gas bill, which was of vital interest to Texas. As a rule the more influential senators spoke little on the floor because their wishes were heard long before legislation reached the stage of formal floor discussion, and Johnson was the prototype of this school. To the outside world Johnson was only a manager of procedure, little concerned with the specific merits of legislation and interested simply in getting the business of the day settled in one fashion or another.

The Senate that Johnson managed with an effectiveness matching that of any of his famous predecessors was an extraordinarily difficult and diverse—and distinguished—assemblage. The period during which I worked in the Senate stands out even in the history of that great institution. The list of personages of past, current, or future prominence is impressive. There were the giants of the past, John Bricker, Alben Barkley and Joe McCarthy. There were the men then enjoying their greatest ascendance, Estes Kefauver, William Knowland, Richard Nixon—who as Vice-President was the Senate's presiding officer—Stuart Symington, Robert Kerr and Richard Russell. And there were the men of the future, Barry Goldwater, John Kennedy, Hubert Humphrey and Lyndon Johnson. They were all men who in one way or another became national figures acting on a stage larger than the Senate chamber. Each (with the exception of McCarthy) was at some time a serious candidate for national elective office. In addition, there were the Senate's own great men, famous as senators because of some special effectiveness in the chamber: Walter George, Styles Bridges, William Fulbright, Paul Douglas, Everett Dirksen, Harry Byrd, Mike Mansfield, Wayne Morse. It would be easy to extend the list further. A Senate boasting such a roster might well stand comparison with any earlier Senate.

The special circumstances of politics in the Eisenhower years also contributed to the Senate's unusual luster. The Senate was controlled by Democrats operating under a Republican executive, which meant that it had an exceptional opportunity to display independence and initiative. Had the President been of the same party, the majority would have been compelled to defer to him more extensively. The Senate in the hands of the Democratic opposition became that party's major rallying point. The Senate was the Democrats' Cave of Adullam, from which they hoped to march forth to national victory. Johnson as Majority Leader devoted his titanic energies to building up that institution, whereas his instinct as President has been naturally to subdue it to the executive will.

The Senate's current eminence as a closely observed national forum and training ground for presidents has disturbed to some extent the institution's traditional intimacy. In conventional images, however, the Senate continues to be portrayed as a "club," where private ceremony takes precedence over public notoriety. There is certainly much truth in such descriptions, though they have never been completely accurate, and have probably become less so since 1956. The Senate has always contained individuals following independent careers either by choice or necessity and the ready access which any senator now has to public attention through television and the press has further encouraged such independence. A senator may have many ends in view other than that of becoming a lifetime member of the Senate's inner circle and consequently may anticipate achieving his ends in ways other than those calculated to please the inner circle.

A senator who declares his independence of the conventional route to power and influence within the Senate can, moreover, choose patterns of conduct calculated to offend senatorial propriety in greater or less degree. Estes Kefauver was the classic example, in my experience, of a senator whose ambitions for national office adversely affected his relations with his colleagues. John Kennedy's tactics were more subtle. Kennedy was a good senator, who avoided unnecessary offense to his superiors, who spoke his mind authoritatively—on selected issues—and who managed successfully to divorce his activities as a national candidate from his conduct on the floor as a respectful junior senator. Kennedy obviously had other things on his mind besides becoming a regular member of the Senate club, but he disengaged himself from its grasp and obligations gingerly and genially.

Johnson and Humphrey, though they turned to national politics from positions of relative strength within the Senate establishment, also achieved their positions in ways far removed from those conventionally assumed to be "correct." The Senate Democrats' choice of Johnson, who served first as Minority Leader and then as Majority Leader from 1953 to 1961, and of Humphrey, who served as Assistant Majority Leader from 1961 to 1965, in fact demonstrates that the Senate's "clubbish" inclinations do not blind it to its need for leaders of competence and national stature. Johnson managed the Senate in accordance with its traditions but apparently felt little personal commitment to them. He was not himself a traditionalist. Humphrey possessed many of the external

18

characteristics of a Northern renegade. He spoke constantly on all subjects and in a tone that suggested that he thought of himself as always addressing a national audience. He seemed to have committed the cardinal sin of carrying his campaign for a national constituency onto the Senate floor itself and of treating the Senate as an audience rather than a club. Yet Humphrey was actually amazingly successful in his personal dealings with the inner circle, for he joined his flamboyance to an irrepressible joviality, which communicated itself to and was ordinarily reciprocated by even his bitterest public rivals. It was generally recognized that Humphrey's manner did not contain a conscious contempt for the Senate's tradition of restraint; it was quite obviously impossible for him to act in any other way.

I never thought to ask myself why I took the trouble to sit down every few days to record what I had seen and heard in and around the Senate floor. It seemed simply a necessary thing to do. My mood was something like that of Thomas Wolfe when he set out to read all the books in the Harvard library and began with "A." The task I set myself was to learn everything. As I learned it, I recorded it. My journal was a sort of private day-to-day report on my progress toward universal knowledge. Periodically I would send extracts from my journal to my family to keep them generally informed of my activities, but the full account I kept to myself.

I was determined to find out what was right and what was real, to pass judgment on the merits of legislation and to describe the foibles of great men in all their startling reality. I listened to the floor debates on pending legislation and decided on that basis what the correct vote would be. My mind was nothing if not open. I felt I had all the necessary material at my disposal and so might as well decide the issues once and for all. At the same time I delighted in anything shocking and sensational. If a senator played a practical joke or said something preposterous, I recorded it faithfully in full. I was fascinated by the unofficial side of Senate life, all those things that never got into the newspapers yet revealed how the Senate functioned on a human level: what senators really thought of one another and how they relaxed and managed to work together.

I was delighted whenever anything embarrassing befell one of the great men I served: No man is *always* a hero to his valet. I seem to have believed, however, that even the worst absurdities and childishness, of the most appallingly obtuse and driveling senator, were something of a tribute to the greatness of the overall institution. I thought it was amazing that such astonishing things could happen right in the middle of the world's greatest deliberative body, but I was equally reassured that the Senate deserved that title for its capacity to take such lapses in stride. I was intrigued, for example, by Joe McCarthy and enjoyed every display of his sinister power. It seemed right for him to be there, for the Senate was designed in my eyes to be a place for dramatic confrontations between good and evil.

I measured the Senate by its capacity to combine extremes and incongruities, quaintness and grandeur, genius and stupidity. The overwhelming impression was of the inexhaustible variety and vitality of the institution, its resilience and resourcefulness. An institution with so much sheer life seemed unlikely to fail to be great. For me, it was a happy experience to spend day after day in a setting where only amazing things happened. At any moment President Sukarno, Vice-President Nixon or Miss Universe might come walking through the door at my elbow.

There are a number of debts I am eager to acknowledge, some old, some more recent. I am first of all grateful to my parents, who disapproved of my leaving home to go to the Senate but who approved of my deciding the question for myself. "My" senator, Earle Clements, helped me in innumerable ways with great generosity. Many members of the Senator's staff, in particular Jeanette Murphy, Pearl Runyon, Frank Dryden, Jack Reed and Henry Ward—and my fellow page Jim Daniel—became good friends and helped to further my education. I am obliged to David Rothman for urging me to dig back into my files in search of the journal whose existence I had almost forgotten after ten years devoted to totally different activities and to Alice and Warren Ilchman and Carolyn Elliott for urging me to pursue its publication.

The text of my journal has been left almost entirely as I found it. It has been slightly condensed by the elimination of some material of purely personal interest. I have occasionally deleted the names of inconsequential senators who have dropped from public consciousness. The initials which have been substituted in such cases have been chosen at random, and are not the actual initials of the senators in question. A few sentences have been altered because their meanings were obscure, but it seemed pointless to attempt extensive revisions. I have few independent memories to confirm or expand what I recorded from day to day in 1956; nor could I write today in the manner I employed eleven years ago. It has seemed advisable, for these and other reasons, to let the text stand as written. To anyone who may have been treated too cavalierly by youthful exuberance, I offer apologies.

The Diary

My living accommodations are ideal. I live overlooking Admiral Farragut, who supposedly said, "Damn the torpedoes! Full speed ahead," or something equally discourteous. It is very difficult to find a statue of anybody in Washington but generals and the like. The Admiral's cannons are very handy for nesting birds. The place is infested with pigeons and squirrels as fat as capitalists.

On my first day I walked all over town finding out where everything is and looking at the exteriors of things. The Washington Monument is rather disappointing, much smaller than it seems on postcards. The memorials to Lincoln and Jefferson, on the other hand, suffer from the postcard treatment. Jefferson's view of the Potomac is magnificent. The most beautiful building externally houses the Federal Reserve; it has much better grounds than the White House, for instance. There is an interesting international Christmas display back of the White House, highlighted by the official tree, from South Dakota, reaching from here to there and with Christmas balls a foot in diameter. As sideshows there are a crèche with live donkeys and all of Santa's reindeer looking the worse for their one-night stand. Dasher, Vixen and Cupid had passed out and were asleep on the hay.

I showed up on schedule at the office of Bobby Baker, Secretary for the Majority, an important position for a man of twenty-seven. On his secretary's desk was a sign that read, "You don't have to be crazy to work here, but it helps." She pressed the green button on her telephone and picked up the receiver. She said, after a minute or so, "Yes, Senator," and then pushed the yellow button and said, "Bill, Senator R. wants a case of White Rock in his office immediately. Oh, and by the way, stop by and pick up some documents while you're at it." Having been sworn in (I am to uphold the Constitution) and being now worth $4,000 in the event of my death (a worthy investment, as Washington drivers drive on the assumption that when the light turns the pedestrian will leap wildly toward the sidewalk), I proceeded to the Democratic cloakroom, where Democratic telephones were being answered by young Democrats. It was 12:02, two minutes after the gavel had first struck, and the sound of 96 senators chortling and backslapping simultaneously was creating quite a racket in the next room. I met the Head Page (wearing a brown suit rather than the customary blue), who said I was the person they had been expecting who didn't fit in anywhere. That was as far as I got the first day, as he said there wasn't much use in my trying to learn anything that day and I should return the next day.

I was sitting in the outer office of the Sergeant at Arms shortly after the breakup of some of the longer New Year's Eve parties waiting for some papers. The secretaries were waiting for one of the six phones to ring while idly sniping at one another. Then a senator burst into the room. I did not know him yet, but he had those unmistakable characteristics, large grin and potbelly. The secretaries instantly girded themselves for joviality. "Say," said one, in her best jolly-good-fellow tone, "that was a wonderful box of candy you sent us up at the office. And do you know who is eating it all up? The chief! Every day he comes in and says, 'Where's that brown box of candy?'—that's yours, Senator." She slapped her thigh in amusement. The Senator slapped his thigh in amusement. Then he burst into the office of the chief, without knocking.

As Senator Humphrey pointed out, the campaign began at 12:35 this afternoon. The State of the Union message was read by a clerk. The President's proposals had been approved by the Senate's 47 Republicans in a meeting in the morning (top secret: only trusted pages allowed). Then followed a short period of bedlam in which each senator was yelling wildly for recognition to insert the speech he had made on the farm problem in Babbling Brook before three thousand people on September 30. After all the smoke had cleared, it was time to hear from the President-Elect of Brazil, who was trying to win friends and influence people. Immediately after the speech Senator Capehart got up to deliver a speech. Simultaneously practically the entire Senate body also arose and left the room. Capehart, earlier in the day, had remarked to Senator B., "I'm going to introduce a new farm-disposal bill." Replied B., "Are you planning to do away with farms altogether?" This question was answered in the speech. He introduced a plan for disposing of surpluses that is not new but perhaps a little more drastic than previous plans. The controversial part of the speech, curiously enough, was his statement that he was not going to blame anyone for the surplus and that he was simply going to accept it as a fact that must be dealt with. It seemed a noble enough sentiment but not to Senator Langer, Republican of North Dakota. He knew exactly whom to blame. He will not vote for a bill proposed by Eisenhower, even for those that are mere formalities, on the grandiose principle that nothing must precede the farm program he advocates. He spent a couple of hours setting his distinguished colleague straight on who was to blame. To the experienced pages this event was old hat. Langer is in rather poor health, and his eyesight and hearing are failing badly, but he pounded a dent in the desk separating him from Senator Capehart, and his voice took on the hoarse quality of a loudspeaker in the small, acoustically marvelous Senate chamber.

The Democrats were gleeful that the distinguished gentleman from North Dakota was turning against the head of his own party, and Senators Morse and Humphrey spent half an hour eulogizing his high principle and integrity. Senator Langer seems to be a very lonely man and less able to cope with his isolation than is Senator Morse, for example. His speech this afternoon seemed to consume angry energy that had been building up for some time. Before and after the speech he was listless. He paid no attention to the praises of the Democrats. He was asked to assume the chair of the Senate, which he did. In the chair he looked very tired. (Once he reportedly said that he would not vote for the confirmation of any ambassador until the appointment of one from North Dakota.)

The rest of the afternoon was spent in a confusing attempt to set the record straight on general subjects by Senators Knowland and Humphrey. One remark that started people buzzing was Knowland's statement that Eisenhower has done such and such "in his first term." Senator Humphrey is an irritating speaker. His high voice carries an accusing, insistent tone, which, added to his repeated references to his own accomplishments, gives him the air of a conceited urchin kicking a servant in the shins. On his round cherubic face his scowls seem incongruous.

On the desk of Mark Trice, Secretary for the Minority, there is the usual collection of elephant ashtrays, elephant flowerpots, elephant paperweights and just plain useless elephants. But the place of honor goes to two egg cups. In each is a golf ball; one had the misfortune to be swatted by Eisenhower, the other by Nixon.

Senator V. is a thoroughly asinine individual. I had been warned of this fact, but it was brought home today. Most senators tolerate interruptions, inquiries and requests for repetition during their speeches. It is only the senators of small mind who make a point of telling people their time is valuable because this is perfectly obvious in the case of an excellent senator. Senator V. is a superb candidate for the category of "Senators of Small Mind." When he was asked to yield the floor for a few minutes so that two minor bills could be taken care of, he first took time to explain that he had been waiting for over an hour and that his committee, which was lost without his invaluable services, was lost at that moment. Then, in an attempt to demonstrate that he was not to be trifled with, he made the incredible statement that he would yield for only one of the two bills. By now all the clerks were smiling with disbelief. Senator Pastore objected but said that he would wait until Hades freezes over if necessary so that the Senator might have a chance to speak. By now all the senators on the floor were laughing heartily, except the distinguished Senator V. He took it as a personal insult, and as a gesture of revenge immediately started in on one of his unbelievably dull speeches. He has a mechanical delivery, in which he emphasizes unusual syllables.

Margaret Chase Smith gave one of her rare floor speeches today in connection with a bill that she introduced proposing a billion dollars for medical research. She, I understand, never speaks without a prepared text. She gave an excellent summary of comparative budgetary trends in medicine, defense and tombstones. The senators always step a little farther out of their accustomed way with Senator Smith. When they ask that she yield the floor, there is always an extra compliment.

Not to be outdone by a subordinate, Nixon also has a golf ball in his Capitol office. It is decorously mounted on a desk set and is a present from the President and Cabinet.

Senator Humphrey made the headlines today by brandishing a copy of *Life* under Secretary Dulles' figurative nose. He quite properly has reason to object to Dulles' rambunctiousness in attempting to bare the United States' teeth when this approach is least desired. Naturally Hubert had to overdo it, using such words as "diabolical" (which he struck from the record) and dragging himself in for the customary pat on the back.

Because of a groundless rumor, seventy Secret Service men were subjected to the trying ordeal of a church service at the National Presbyterian on January 14 to protect our President.

The numbers in the Senate Office Building go up to 463. The number of Senator McCarthy's office is 463. I saw the Senator for the first time today. He is short and pudgy, built a little like Senator Knowland, that is, with no neck. This build gives him the appearance of great power. He is swarthy, with long arms and a black suit, which, along with his tentative movements, gives him something of the air of a spider. It is hard to tell at this time what his rating is with other senators. Everyone greeted him at least civilly. Lyndon Johnson came over to shake hands. But there is none of the hearty bonhomie that is usually present. When he approached two senators engaged in conversation in the back of the chamber, there seemed to be a slight hesitation in his movements. He evidently is well liked personally by the pages. In manner he is mild and pleasant, despite his appearance of latent power.

January 20, 1956

The senators from the gas-producing states, Monroney of Oklahoma, Fulbright of Arkansas and Daniel of Texas, to name a few, all presented excellent arguments in favor of the natural-gas bill. Their argument is that all Gaul is divided into three parts, the producer, the pipeline, and the city distributor. Senators Pastore and Douglas contend that all Gaul is divided into four parts, the fourth being the consumer. Lyndon Johnson, in an eloquent speech, his first open advocacy of any measure in this session, said it was a question of whether or not we trust the capitalistic system. On all sides it has been a magnificent debate with all the Senate's really fine men making their first debating appearances of the session. Senator Pastore is a strange man with black hair and a moustache. He has a sickly grin; he bares his teeth and utters something resembling a death rattle. He can be very vehement. It is almost comical to see Pastore and Douglas, leaders of the opposition to the gas bill, together. Pastore, small and dark, is about half the size of the majestic, white-haired Douglas. The debate has been a great strain on Douglas, who has shown magnificent poise, courtesy and restraint.

I can now boast of having seen Congressman Tumulty of New Jersey, who weighs more than 350 pounds and whose stomach arrives approximately two feet before he enters the room officially. If Douglas and Pastore form a strange contrast, that formed by "Tummy" and Senator Clifford Case is even more pronounced.

The Congressman appeared a couple of feet wider beside the gaunt Senator Case.

It is an excellent custom to have freshmen senators do most of the presiding over the Senate. It familiarizes them with Senate procedures and with their fellow senators and does not cut out a senior senator from his debating on the floor. The presiding officers usually have very little idea of what is going on and merely repeat the official words whispered to them by the Parliamentarian.

The big event of January 19 was a two-hour smear of Dulles by Republican Jenner of Indiana. He said that the Secretary was well-known for deceit and that his recent bellicose attitude is merely a front to hide a weak-kneed retreat before the Communists. He decried attempts to bathe the heathen when the heathen will not fall in with our military ambitions and do not live up to our time-honored principles.

Senator Humphrey showed today (January 20) that he still has plenty of spleen to vent. Two other speeches were also made on the "Case of the Blundering Secretary." Neely of West Virginia delivered an unashamed smear. Mike Mansfield of Montana gave a sober analysis, saying that the Democratic policies adopted by the Eisenhower administration were applicable until world conditions changed. At one point in his speech, he said, "I believe Mr. Dulles is an honorable man." I expected him to say, "So are they all—all honorable men." Humphrey showed himself on the side of ire by praising Neely, while questioning Mansfield.

I learned the other day how it was possible for Wayne Morse to break the filibuster record a year or two ago with a speech of almost 23 hours. He whiled away the hours by discussing how he courted his wife and how his ten-year-old daughter was doing in school and by reading letters from constituents. He would say, "Now here is an example of just what we've been discussing in regard to this bill." Then he would read an article from *Reader's Digest* about the hazards of being a milkman or "How I Became a Forger."

29

I had asked Senator Alben Barkley to autograph a picture as an excuse for introducing myself, and he was in the process of doing so outside the chamber when he was approached by an interesting person. They shook hands. Mr. Barkley said, "How do you do, Mr. Bowles?" When he had left and while the former Vice-President was signing, I asked him, "Is that Chester Bowles, former Ambassador to India?" He nodded. "I understand he was very popular but the present Ambassador is also very popular." Barkley assented good-naturedly.[1]

Later, introducing myself as a Kentuckian, I asked Mr. Bowles his opinion of the work of his successor Cooper. He said he thought that Cooper was doing a splendid job. He added that he was to meet with Cooper in the morning. On returning to the rostrum, I said to one of the pages, intending to impress him with an account of my meeting with the famous Ambassador, "Do you know who is out in the hall?" "Yes," he replied, "Miss Universe. I already have her autograph. You can get it if you want. She's in the President's Room." I rushed to the President's Room, forgetting Chester Bowles. Miss Universe, whose illegible autograph I secured, is rather attractive, has lovely blond hair and is at least five feet ten. Her picture was taken with the pages. When one of the pages remarked that they went to school at 6:30 in the morning she said "Oooooo," blinking her eyes demurely and smiling at the cameras. It is no doubt significant that she added her phone number to the autograph.

I have the following tale on good authority: One day last year when Senator Q. was feeling his Cheerios (or something equally potent) he happened to drive down a streetcar underpass, mistak-

---

[1] The incumbent Ambassador was John Sherman Cooper, the Republican whom Barkley had defeated in his bid for re-election to the Senate in 1954. Barkley, who had been Vice-President until 1953, served in the Senate from 1955 until his death in 1956. In the election following Barkley's death, Cooper regained the seat he had lost, resigning his ambassadorship upon Eisenhower's request that he run. Chester Bowles later returned to *his* former position as Ambassador to India during the Kennedy-Johnson administrations.

ing it for the entrance to the senators' private garage. He yelled at a passing streetcar, "Hey, this is for senators only."

While we're on the subject of errant senators, I will add an anecdote whispered to me as Senator Douglas swung into the last fifty pages of his four-day speech. One day last year Senator Y. was drinking in the cloakroom, and two pages were standing chatting nearby. He suddenly threw the water in his glass up in the air, and, when it descended in the general vicinity of the two pages, he unconcernedly stuck out his hand and commented, "I think the roof is leaking." The pages, not to be outdone, brought a special rush communication to the Senator, which consisted of a large envelope containing a water pistol. Senator Y. tested it out on a dozen senators earnestly talking together nearby. It worked.

Just to indicate how much things cost in Washington, it cost me 60 cents to go to a movie to which I had a pass, given to me by the Secretary for the Minority. This expense consisted of streetcar fare and tax. I am rolling in dough, however, and was a little amused at Daddy's offer to send me some money. Just yesterday I sent a check for $73 to the bank. My new room is $30 a month. It is very satisfactory and as cheap as can be found in Washington. I eat my noon meal at about 11:15—the Senate begins at 12:00—and generally stock up well on low-priced food at the Senate cafeteria, run for senators and employees only. At night I eat at one of half a dozen not too expensive restaurants on Pennsylvania Avenue.

This Sunday one of the pages (from Montana) is taking me to the President's church, the National Presbyterian. I will have attended Community, Episcopalian, Lutheran and Presbyterian churches on the first four Sundays. By the way, on the same day that I met Chester Bowles and Miss Universe, the Prince of the Netherlands was introduced to the Senate.

The natural-gas bill has now seen nine days of debate come and crawl away in sad condition. After the first week I was outlining the speeches before they were given. But to begin at the beginning. What the bill proposes to do is to free natural-gas producers from their present control by the Federal Power Commission. They were thus free before 1954, when a Supreme Court decision put them under Federal jurisdiction. The present Harris-Fulbright

31

bill is an attempt by the gas-producing states to restore the earlier situation. The case for the affirmative was presented by three representatives of gas states, Monroney of Oklahoma, Fulbright of Arkansas and Long of Louisiana. They began by insisting that the producer was not the determiner of price, that it actually was the city distributor who hiked up the price. They showed that the producer only got 10 percent of the consumer's dollar. And then followed three contentions:

1. There was no price increase between 1938 and 1954 when there was no control.

2. Since there is at present a great demand for gas, the demand can best be met by speculators encouraged by the hope of greater profits to search out wells. This will actually stabilize the market and in the long run mean lower prices, they argue.

3. The bill is favored by the Federal Power Commission, the regulating body, and has the sanction of a Cabinet committee.

The opposition, Senators Pastore and Douglas, countered with two main arguments. First, they said the gas industry was inherently liable to Federal control (a) because a small group of 197 producers control 90 percent of the market and (b) because the 26 million households using natural gas have invested $11 billion in equipment and are thus captive consumers. The consumer has therefore no choice but to pay whatever the gas company asks because by discarding his gas equipment he would be throwing away a large investment. And so, when Senator Fulbright argues that if the gas price goes too high the consumer need not buy it, Senator Douglas says it is the same as saying that if the phone rates go too high the customer can always use carrier pigeons or shout loudly through an open window. He adds that gas is different from coal or other commodities in that there is only one method of distribution—pipeline—and once the consumer is hooked up to a producer, these bonds are next to indissoluble; the entire industry must be regulated, not just one-third of it. Douglas compares dividing it to Solomon's suggestion that the baby be cut in half to please the disputing mothers. The first argument is that the industry is monopolistic in nature because a few companies control the market, because the customer has invested so much money in gas equipment and because gas has only one means of transportation.

32

From there the opposition goes more directly counter to the claims of the affirmative: Even though the industry may be monopolistic, is there need for regulation if during sixteen years there was no price increase without controls? Senator Douglas argues that these figures are immaterial, for the industry has grown tremendously in the past few years, and there is today a seller's market. There are thousands of people in Chicago alone on waiting lists for gas. Douglas contends that regulation is needed especially at this time when, due to the great demand, the producers could charge all that the traffic will bear. But won't this deficit be made up when there is greater impetus to producers in the way of profits to find gas? Senator Douglas points out that under Federal regulation there was no slackening in the number of speculators and that the producers have certain very liberal tax advantages. For these reasons he insists that no greater enticement is needed. And he has a wealth of statistical data to show it. The opposition thus contends that the industry is basically monopolistic and that regulation is needed especially at the present time because of the abnormal market conditions.

This is the way I summarized the first thirty hours or so of debate, what I sifted from the four-day speech of Senator Douglas, the barrage of statistics, charts, challenges, inferences and so forth. And I thought that there was very little left to say on the subject. So I was interested to see what would happen in the next few speeches. I was pleased to find that my outline of the debate was correct. This was first shown in the speech of Senator Kennedy, boy wonder from Massachusetts. Practically everyone fainted with surprise when he sat down after speaking only twenty minutes. He summarized the arguments of the negative, precisely as I had already outlined them. His speech was timely, coming as it did immediately after the exhaustive treatment of Senator Douglas. It put the real issues back into focus.

The next day I found Senator Humphrey also conforming to my outline of the arguments of Senator Douglas. He said in his speech that "any of us who follow him can only reiterate what the distinguished Senator from Illinois has said." He also made a penetrating remark when he said, "as I will point out again for purposes of repetition." There seemed to be little point to the debate except repetition. I suppose in the coming elections everyone wants to be able to say that he said such and such in the debate on this issue.

Being thoroughly acquainted with the facts in the case through Senator Douglas' speech, I was in a better position to judge the debating that followed. First, Humphrey took on Senator Long. Long tried to establish the point, already stated, that more profit incentive was needed to increase the supply of natural gas. It is a weak argument, as Senator Douglas' figures show that the producers are already receiving special tax treatment. Humphrey was able to get the best of him. Later in the afternoon, however, Senator Monroney took up the cudgel. I had felt all along that the most convincing argument for the affirmative was the support of the bill by the Federal Power Commission. It is the one point to which the opposition has no answer. So I was a little surprised that the affirmative did not pound this home properly at first. And when Senator Monroney took this tangent against Humphrey, he was able to force the Senator from Minnesota to back down and stammer something about maybe we need a new Commission.

Senator Douglas has been the master of the debate from the beginning. You get the feeling now that the teacher is sitting back and watching the pupil run through his memorized paces as the debate rolls on. Humphrey has been doing a good job on the whole, considering that he is laboring under the handicap of an unpleasant voice. He is always sticking out his pointed chin, which juts from an otherwise pudgy face.

Most of the debate has been put on by the negative. This is because it is almost a foregone conclusion that the bill will pass. And so the affirmative has not exerted itself to the point of exhaustion as has the Senator from Illinois.

I have absolutely no prejudice in the matter, knowing nothing whatever about the issue except what I have heard on the floor. Both sides have very strong cases, and so the presentation of individual senators will be the deciding point. By "deciding" I mean who comes off better in the debate. The bill is already decided. The majority of senators have listened to very little of the debate. Douglas said that the reason for his speech was that he thought that there were about twenty thousand readers of the *Congressional Record* and he considered these people the formers of public

34

opinion. His concern is public information rather than to persuade senators. He could do that much more easily by personal talks.

Douglas is a masterly debater. Of course there are some people who think that little is accomplished in four days that could not be thrashed out in an hour or two. He presented a mass of authoritative material for the *Record* and sparred with Monroney for hours. Monroney is also a very sharp debater, and both have remarkable senses of humor. Douglas once referred to Senator Anderson as a "very prosperous farmer." Anderson objected, saying that the farm situation was so bad that he could hardly pay his way. Douglas replied, "Am I to understand that the Senator operates a very large farm purely for the sake of psychic income?"

I am now in possession of what may be a highly significant document. It is a bill on which Senator Joseph McCarthy was doodling while waiting to be recognized to make a statement about the Ukrainian underground. I have given it a cursory psychoanalytical examination, and I have decided the figures are either ghosts or Ku Klux Klanners, all of whom are holding hands. This, I deduce, indicates his subconscious willingness to use underhand methods.

The gas debate will probably go on for another week, for everyone wants to be able to tell the home folks that their particular interests have been represented. From the initial struggle of the session, I am beginning to feel the dividing line between those senators who are only interested in the political fences back home and those who really have a sincere interest in problems more far-reaching in nature. For instance the speech Senator S. gave on the gas bill was entirely on how it would affect his home state. But Douglas has only mentioned Illinois incidentally, when he has happened to use a figure connected with his home state because he is more familiar with the situation at home.

Senator Clements' duties as Assistant Majority Leader are basically these: He is a member of the Democratic Policy Committee (9 members). He, with Majority Leader Lyndon Johnson and a couple of others, formulates Democratic party strategy, and then the two leaders try to get the rest of the party to fall into line on major issues. Clements spends most of his time on the floor talking with senators individually or in small groups. So far he has spoken officially only on matters of routine business ("Mr. President, I move that the journal of the previous day's proceedings be approved without reading").

He has three men in his office who assist him directly. One is his administrative assistant, who has general office duties and is a specialist in agriculture. The second is his legislative assistant, who is a lawyer. He drafts bills and takes care of correspondence of a legal nature. The third is something called "legislative aide," and he says he isn't sure himself what he does.

I learned today that Senator X.'s page R. not only was accustomed to use marijuana back home but also has just received a shipment and "You should have seen me last night." The shipment cost $20. One cigarette costs $1.50. As though prophetically, on the same day $50,000 worth of the evil weed was carted up to the President's Room for pictures in connection with some kind of article. I asked R. why he takes the stuff, especially when it costs so much. He said that it makes you feel so happy. Everyone laughs at the drop of a hat, everyone has fun. He says it is not at all habit-forming, and he could stop any time he wanted to.

John Sherman Cooper dropped into the Senate chamber today. He said that he had not had a single day off since he assumed his ambassadorial duties in India. He said that there was a great deal of pomp and ceremony connected with his job, which the Indians had come to expect during their period under British control. This ceremoniousness was much greater than he had experienced in the Senate.

January 27, 1956

Secretary of Agriculture Benson stuck both feet in his mouth today. The official issue of the day was still the gas bill, but the debate was generating little interest among senators and even less among press correspondents; the debate lacked the color of Douglas and the choler of Pastore. Senator Humphrey, maintaining his position as chief rabble-rouser, first opened the subject of Benson

36

in a fiery speech, which revealed these basic facts: In the December issue of *Harper's* an article on the farm situation appeared. It claimed that the farmer was being pampered by both political parties and that he was beginning to expect this treatment. In a remark reminiscent of Wilson's famous "bird-dog, kennel-dog" statement, the article said that, when a hog has had its jowls in the trough too long, it begins to think that the trough belongs to it. It suggested gently nudging a million farmers off the farms into other profitable employment. Humphrey said that *he* had never advocated getting rid of the farm problem by getting rid of the farmers. The article concluded by suggesting using up surplus eggs by throwing them at political candidates who posed as the farmers' friends in the next elections. This article was sent to Secretary Benson, and the following letter appeared in the February issue of *Harper's:* "I have read the article and consider it excellent. Ezra Taft Benson."

At this point in the remarks of the Senator from Minnesota, Democrats were throwing their hats in the air and laughing. Republicans were turning red in the face. Reporters were piling into the press gallery. Republicans Francis Case of South Dakota and Young of North Dakota, two gentlemen conservative in thought and speech, collectively hit the roof. Young called the article "uncouth." Case said that the Secretary had compromised his usefulness to the point at which he was a hindrance to the President and should resign. Case is a mousy little man who previously had displayed little character. But today eloquence was flowing from all sorts of unexpected places. That was as far as things got for the moment, as Senator Lehman returned to his speech on gas. Republicans, reeling, were meeting in small stunned groups to recoup. Senator Case said: "I understand since there has been so much adverse criticism of Benson he has what amounts to a form letter which he sends out to any publication which doesn't smear him. He is so eager for some good words he jumped too fast on this one."

The first official Republican reply came quite properly from the ranking member of the Senate Agriculture Committee, Senator Aiken of Vermont, who always wears red bow ties. The Senator said that, upon checking with the Secretary, he had discovered that Benson had not seen the article; he had not seen or signed the letter of congratulations; a subordinate had signed his name, something not unusual; upon hearing of the substance of the article he was quite opposed to it; he, however, accepted full responsibility as head of the Department for what he termed a "boner." This full statement of the facts in the case instigated the second round of attacks.

Senator Long, who had not previously heard of the "boner," was laughing delightedly at the back of the chamber. Humphrey, chortling with evil glee, returned to the attack. He said that it is a strange administrator who has people under him who would so go against his wishes. He intimated that the subordinate was actually carrying out the wishes of the Secretary. He said that he could take the statement "I have read the article" only at its face value. He said that he would never authorize such a statement if it were false.

No one ventured forth with real vigor to defend Mr. Benson. Senator Knowland read a formal statement of apology written by the Secretary (presumably). Someone made a few hedging remarks to the effect that the country would be a lot better off if the energy expended in partisan attacks were used in forming constructive legislation. But Senators Humphrey and Long waltzed gaily out of the chamber unscathed and unabashed.

Republican hopes, though a shambles on one field of battle, may still advance on another. Senator Neuberger reportedly said that the Republicans might stoop to using drugs to keep the President apparently fit during the next campaign. Senators Goldwater and Knowland were more correct when they found Neuberger guilty of the stooping in the case.

The latest word on the gas bill is that it will pass with a margin of from five to ten votes. The word is from Bobby Baker, Secretary for the Majority, than whom there is no one more in the know. This was one of the miscellaneous bits of information I garnered while in his office. He is a very agreeable person with a "Suthun" accent, who knows everything about everyone and everything. He is twenty-seven. He took time out today to urge me to go into law. He said if I don't want to be a doctor or a minister that would be the most satisfying profession. He said that the greatest men he has known are those in whom brilliance of mind is joined to practicality. He said that Senator A. failed miserably as a senator because he was "too goddam brilliant." He was unable to come through with a realization of the practicalities of life. So much for one young man who is rising rapidly.

I spent a couple of hours today finding out that it would take a great deal longer than that to exhaust the possibilities of the Museum of Natural History of the Smithsonian. I saw Jerry the Rhinoceros and walked under a 78-foot whale. I learned later that I was elevating myself in the wrong cathedral of knowledge: Ike had spent the afternoon in the Mellon Art Gallery.

Take the *Iliad*, the *Odyssey*, the *Aeneid*; add $6 million and a clear Hollywood conscience, and you get *Helen of Troy*, currently at the Metropolitan Cinema. Just as everything that happened during the Civil War happened to Scarlett O'Hara in *Gone with the Wind*, so everything in the Trojan war was a direct result of the valor of Paris and the treachery of Ulysses, whom Vergil calls "that crime-contriving bastard." Spread over thousands of square feet of screen were thousands of square Trojans, their faces glowing with native color and passion. King Priam stares into the depths of Helen's soul and says with deep passion, "This is the face that launched a thousand ships." It gives me a strange feeling to go into a Washington movie theater and not just because it costs 90 cents rather than 30 cents. The news is less than a week old, and I have always been used to the two-month-old flashes at home. I get an uncomfortable feeling that the news is breathing down my neck. Newsreels at home are always relaxing.

January 30, 1956

The paper reported today that the President and Mrs. Eisenhower attended church services at the National Presbyterian Church. It neglected to mention the fact that I was there too. I sat a row behind and about forty feet away from the President. In the flesh he does not seem as tall as the photographs make him, and his baldness is more noticeable. Yet he does not look at all like a man recovering from a heart attack. He pranced out of the church, and Mamie could hardly keep up with him. For a while I thought the Secret Service man behind him was reverently saying a prayer, but it turned out that he was only chewing gum. The sermon was preached by a man from Minneapolis, and I wholeheartedly disagreed with most of the things he said. The choir and solos were terrific. But I must admit that most of the effect was lost on me. It seemed for all the world like going to the theater. We all lined up before the church, and we had to be there early to get a seat. The President wore glasses through most of the service, taking them off for entrance and exit. Mamie had a pair of glasses on a stalk that you hold on your nose. I have now been to the Vice President's church (Westmoreland), Sherman Adams' church (St. John's) and the chruch of the President and John Foster Dulles (National Presbyterian). I hope to go soon to Peter Marshall's church.

The streetcar that goes by my door on East Capitol is a most miraculous one. It goes past half a dozen movie theaters and most of the famous churches, among other places, so when I want to go anywhere I take it. It has a most uneven course, but it seems to go down the right streets.

The pages certainly can't complain about the publicity they receive. A couple of years ago they went on a spree and broke a couple of streetlights, and it was in every paper in the country. And so far I have been photographed with Miss Universe (!) and in connection with an article to appear in the *Portland Oregonian* and centered around Senator Neuberger's page. We were photographed looking at a variety of oddments in the Smithsonian and at the paintings that cost Andrew Mellon over $1,600,000, which are in the National Art Gallery.

I was much elated to have the chance to exchange a few words today with Soapy Williams, famous Governor of Michigan and prominently mentioned candidate for the Vice-Presidency on the Democratic ticket. He said that he had been very cordially received by Governor Wetherby of Kentucky. He has a wonderful

40

smiling face and dark eyebrows that give him some of the Billy Graham appearance. I'm beginning to feel as though the mountain were coming to Mohammed.

Senator Morse gave his first oration of the session today. He is against the gas bill. But in my opinion his objections are based on a fallacious assumption. It was a Supreme Court interpretation that put the producers under Federal control in 1954. Morse asserts that to enact the present legislation would actually be overruling the Supreme Court, which would endanger the separation of powers. The distinction he fails to see is that there would be no overruling because a new law is being passed, which is a fully legitimate function. The Supreme Court was not declaring an irrevocable policy but was applying the legislation provided it by the Congress. So no overruling would be involved in providing the Court with new legislation to interpret. There are varying reactions to Morse around the Senate. When he received the Sidney Hillman award, my Republican reactionary page friend said that it should have been the Benedict Arnold award. Yet others think him one of the Senate's brilliant men. He can be a vicious speaker at times. During the Benson brawl he said, "I always knew he was a short-sighted reactionary, but I didn't know he was a fool." And some of his remarks, like his initial statement that "I will fight this bill," are delivered dripping with pure venom. He can speak for hours, a fact he made amply clear today, and always appear dapper and fresh.

February 1, 1956

Although the gas argument is generally threadbare by now, two of the most interesting speeches on the subject were delivered today (February 1). Senator D. got all hot and bothered and used bad English and had excruciating pronunciation. I almost burst out laughing when he started talking about the "figgers." He reduced the entire debate to a cliché and spent an hour repeating himself. It was his contention that the consumer isn't worried about whether or not the producer raises his price; he's interested

41

in keeping baby's bottle warm and in keeping the home fires burning under the morning pancakes. So he advocated the bill to induce the producers to search for more gas instigated by the hope of greater profit. He kept repeating the refrain "two cents a day," which he said the producer was now getting. He said it is unimportant what the poor gas producers (sixth largest United States industry) charge because it's only two cents a day and even if they raised the price Mama would still be able to warm baby's bottle.

The other speech of note was the first address of the session by Senator Dirksen, the only true orator the Senate possesses. He would not be caught dead using simple English. Although everyone else has been using the term "city distributors" for the pipeline companies in town, Senator Dirksen talked of "purveyors within the city." When Dirksen speaks, the only thing to do is sit back and let his golden voice undulate softly over you. He speaks from the diaphragm. He dismissed the topic at hand in about five minutes, supporting the gas bill. From there he leapt into the realms of the imagination. He said that this bill was in the great pioneering spirit. How could anyone be so callous as to believe our noble business fraternity, the gas producers, capable of gouging the consumers? Where is their trust in the great American system? By now the bill's opponents were cringing in their seats and calling themselves no good.

It is seldom that a speaker will deviate to any extent from a prepared statement except in direct exchanges on the floor. Dirksen came with a scrap of paper with a few scribbled notes to deliver his oration. It is delicious to hear him mouth such gems as "instrumentalities" and make a beautiful sound of "impracticable." It is obvious that Dirksen just loves to speak, loves the sound of "wuuuurds." But he is a great enough orator not to appear fatuous or bloated. He gravely and sadly spoke of the "impolite" language being exchanged between Democrats on the issue. At the end of the first hour, when everyone in the chamber was hanging onto his every golden syllable, he said that if there were no more speakers for the day he would be willing to "visit" with the Senate indefinitely. Unfortunately Senator Langer just happened to have a little matter of 93 pages he wished to get over with. So Dirksen pulled all the golden images he had cast forth into a neat little package clinching his argument about the universal character of Eisenhower with a story from the Bible. Somebody constructed a body from flesh and bones, but it was immobile until God told him to blow the breath of the four winds into it and make a people. Not two, not half a dozen, but a people. Thus Eisenhower blows the breath of uniting spirit into the people of the United States. Dirksen gave the most gripping speech I have heard. I was reluctant to miss a syllable of the hour-long speech. It acted like a tonic. Senator Langer is almost totally blind. The reading clerks took turns with his 93-page condemnation of Harry Dexter White of the Truman era.

I have discovered the reason why any senator appearing on television is shown before a window out of which can be seen the Capitol dome. In the Capitol's basement studios is a window with a large picture of the Capitol behind it.

February 2, 1956

The latest mountain to pay homage to humble Mohammed is the Prime Minister of Great Britain. Today was Sir Anthony Day in the Senate, and very little business was done. The Senate adjourned at the unheard-of hour of 2:00 P.M., giving us hard-working little beavers a break. We have been having an unbroken string of sessions lasting until 6:00 or 7:00. Considerable interest was generated by Eden's visit, and outside the packed galleries there was a line of some proportions. Chairs were set on the floor of the Senate for distinguished ambassadors, and a solid wall of senatorial assistants lined the back of the chamber. For the first time what might be called a respectable quorum of senators was present. The only ones whose absence I spotted were Eugene Millikin, who is hospitalized, and good ole Joe McCarthy. Eden came in the wrong door so I found myself stationed in the wrong place, but this error was quickly corrected, and I had a fine view of him through his fifteen-minute address. He is much easier to understand than Churchill or the Queen. He used few gestures, but they were effective. He did not vary his voice quality but spoke with moderation and force. When he had reached the end of his prepared statement and while the reporters were already halfway out the door, he began speaking off the cuff, with much better results. He is ineffably everything a Britisher is supposed to be. He is almost as tall as his two escorts, Senators Johnson and Knowland, but not nearly so florid and healthy-looking. He seemed especially pale and anemic beside the bulk of Knowland. His immaculately groomed, swept-back graying hair; his moustache, emphasizing his receding chin, and everything about him were startlingly British. He was gracious and at ease and humorous, saying that he would not receive such a wholehearted welcome in the House of Commons.

After his speech he just had time to shake hands with 94 senators and 20 pages. This time we were on the right side of the chamber, and the Democratic pages almost missed the whole show. While he was shaking hands, he laughed and swayed back and forth from foot to foot. His hand was soft and limp. When he had finished shaking hands with all the pages and just as Lyndon Johnson was signaling that it was time to head for the House of Representatives, the Prime Minister called to the pages to come back, that he wanted to talk to them. He asked what we did; we said we trotted bills around. "Do you have any connection with the other house?" he asked. "No," we said. "I suppose you're always fighting with the chaps over there," he joked. He added: "I suppose you will all become senators. Is that the system?" We assured him that was the general idea. In conclusion he said that he thought pages were a "jolly good idea" and that he would have to look into the matter for the pageless British government. By this time Lyndon Johnson was scratching his head in bewilderment, but he finally dragged Sir Anthony away. This interview had a profound effect on one of the pages. "Gosh," he said, "I sure have more respect for the British Government."

Senator Goldwater, Chairman of the Republican Senatorial Campaign Committee, started walking a tightrope carrying a barrel of boiling water the other day when he introduced a bill making it illegal for unions to contribute to political parties. It didn't take long for that boiling water to start spilling over in counter-charges by George Meany. If Goldwater is really serious, and it's a little late now for him to decide he isn't (the unions have pledged $3 million to defeat eleven members of Congress, one of whom is Barry Goldwater), the attempt to bar union funds might become the first strictly partisan issue of the campaign year.

P.S.: Gas vote next Monday. Then without pause the sugar bill, to import more sugar, which will be opposed by sugar-producing states. The Senate usually doesn't start moving like this (in continuous sessions) until April.

February 7, 1956

It's too bad, but Maureen will have to forget about being a page. I understand that a delegation of hefty young damsels recently came down to see Margaret Chase Smith about the possibility of her sponsoring a female page. She refused.

One senator remarked to another during the gas debate that he was going over to his office because he thought there would be less gas there. His friend replied, "Are you sure there will be, once you get there?"

Senator Dirksen wandered in today with a briefcase full of handkerchiefs for Senator Goldwater, Chairman of the Republican Senatorial Campaign Committee. The handkerchiefs were embroidered with the letters "Y-C-E-R-B-S-O-Y-A." They have not divulged the secret to the Democrats yet, but the handkerchiefs now being worn by several Republicans actually convey the message that "you can't elect Republicans by sitting on your ass."

I suppose it is axiomatic that news rarely comes from expected places and that attention is hardly ever attracted by the most diligent people. Senator Douglas said that he had worked six months compiling material on the gas bill. Senators Monroney and Fulbright have always been familiar with the gas industry and its problems. But it took Senator Francis Case of South Dakota to catapult the gas controversy into the headlines. It was the leading headline for several days in the Washington area. The axiom could be extended to read, "news rarely happens at the expected time." Everyone was expecting to close up shop around the chamber about 2:00 and get set for a marathon session on Monday lasting from 10:00 in the morning way into the night in an effort to get rid of the bill once and for all. The motion to recess was just about to be made when up pops Case. "I rise to make a difficult speech. I had not expected to take part in the debate on this pending legislation . . . I know very little about the economics in the collection and distribution of natural gas. I speak, therefore, only because one phase of the matter before us has presented itself to me in an unsought and unavoidable manner. . . . Had this incident not happened I suppose that I would have followed the course recommended by the overwhelming majority of telegrams and letters from my state and voted for the bill." Here is the story he unfolded. He had made public statements saying that he favored the aims of the bill and that, if he did not find objections to the technicalities of the bill, he would vote for it. An out-of-state lawyer, whose name he did not divulge, upon ascertaining his stand, gave to a person in South Dakota 25 $100 bills for the Senator's campaign fund. This person called the Senator. The Senator instructed him to whom to give the money. When it was discovered that the money came from an out-of-state lawyer who had inquired about his stand on the gas bill, it was "deduced" that the lawyer was representing gas interests and that the money was an expression of gratitude for his vote on the bill.

Now a fairly anonymous campaign contribution of $2,500 may seem insignificant when it is charged that the bill may cost the consumer $800 million and when the figures show that $14 billion have been invested in gas equipment. But it is the first concrete evidence of something that has been preying on the minds of many senators: that there may possibly be more in this bill than is proper for the mammoth gas companies. Case said that there certainly must be the prospect of some mighty large profits later if the companies could afford such down payments. These doubts were real enough to cause the chief proponents, Fulbright and Monroney, to consider this speech a man-sized stumbling block in the way of the passage of the bill, and they rushed to the attack. Fulbright pointed out that this sum has actually influenced a vote of a senator, as Case was previously going to vote for the bill, and he suggested that the money might possibly have come from one of the opponents of the bill. He called eleven times for the immediate release of the name of the person so that the Senate might get to the heart of the matter. Case refused to tell and admitted privately that he was not sure of the origin of the money. Things kept getting hotter. Monroney, one of the Senate's most genial personalities, at one point said flatly, "I resent that." The Senate was recessed so that some fancy maneuvering might be accomplished. Then things really started getting interesting. Case, a small, normally mild man with a high voice; Styles Bridges; Bill Knowland, and Lyndon Johnson got together in the Republican cloakroom. Now, when the Senate is not in session, reporters are allowed on the Senate floor. So they were racing for the cloakroom like a pack of wolves toward a rabbit hole. I was stationed to keep them out of one door, and one of our supervisors was stationed at the other. The reporters licked their chops and waited. So did I. Case was on one side of the room, sitting forward tensely and twisting a typewriter eraser nervously in his hands. The others sat opposite him. Senator Bricker was lying on a couch, keeping a sleepy eye on what was transpiring. Afterwards, Johnson said to reporters that he was meeting with Knowland in the morning to discuss such things as an investigation and a possible postponement of the vote. This was all, and, as one reporter said, there was nothing really pithy in what he said. Knowland, bursting into a fast sprint, was able to leave reporters behind.

This incident re-emphasized the vast amount of propaganda going around about this bill. Full-page advertisements have been appearing in *The Washington Post* asking senators to vote against the bill. Senator Goldwater said that he hoped that they would have the vote soon, before all the publicity started taking effect. Hourly broadcasts are being beamed over the radio stations of Maryland against the bill. Both Maryland senators support it. The matter of 25 $100 bills would be unimportant by itself; it is the vast quantity of lobbying of which they are an indication that makes the matter important.

Well, Monday's vote is past (53–38), and, as it turned out, the Case case created more stir in the newspapers and in the stock market (Phillips down 1 3/8) than in the Senate itself. Of course, a select and distinguished committee (Senators George, Hayden, Bridges, Thye) with a budget of $10,000 was appointed to investigate the incident involving $2,500. But it seems that naming this committee is only to pacify the public, for it was revealed that the money came from private sources and not from gas companies, and there seemed little law-breaking involved. It did not affect the vote on the bill. And the senators, if they were concerned with it at all, merely joked about it. When Senator E. mentioned to McCarthy that it seemed a great deal of fuss about a small sum of money, Joe replied, "Yes, the price is low out there." And the cloakroom comment generally seemed to be that the controversy had no relation to the merits or demerits of the bill.

It took eleven hours, from 10:00 A.M. to 9:00 P.M., to dispose of the bill. The Senate was working under a special agreement, which limited debate on each proposed amendment to one hour and on final passage to three hours. A couple of senators introduced amendments proposing to insert a comma somewhere just to be able to speak for a while about the bill; they later withdrew their amendments. Yet there were about six votes during the day on various serious attempts to alter the final form of the bill. All attempts were defeated. More than ninety senators voted on each amendment, so there was a whole horde sitting around in the cloakroom waiting for a vote most of the time. That meant that the pages hardly had a chance to sit down. Before each vote most of the senators wanted a roll-call sheet or, as Senator Flanders said, a "scorecard." We distributed them. And then there are the innumerable small things. I called Merrill Lynch Pierce Fenner & Beane to find out for Senator Goldwater how the gas stocks were reacting to the Case case.

The Senate staff rolls into high gear as a vote approaches and as it proceeds. Beside having to keep a running tally of the vote to see how our side is doing and whether an extra effort might just swing it, the Secretary for the Minority and the pages are dashing around wildly trying to get the senators there in time for the vote. I grab one phone and call the offices of a dozen or so senators in swift succession to tell them to run over as fast as they can while one of the other pages is doing the same thing on another phone. It's really very funny to watch the senators stalling to allow a colleague to pant into the chamber in time to record his vote. Once the Clerk has gone through all the names, everyone gets up and asks the chair how he is recorded as voting. Telling twenty or thirty senators how they are recorded as voting usually allows the five or so minutes necessary for the tardy to make it.

When an important bill like this one comes up, the Vice-President has to stay pretty close to the chamber. It is ironic that there was only one tie vote in the last session, and on that occasion the Vice-President could not be located. I saw more of him on Monday than I had all year. He had just returned from Brazil and was not in tremendously good humor. An indication was his even more than usually vigorous use of the gavel. He is the loudest gaveler that ever I have heard. I jump six inches every time he brings it down. It was he who broke the gavel that had been in use in the Senate since the first Congress met. A facsimile carved from ivory, a present of the Indian government, is now used, and the patched-up old one occupies a symbolic position on the rostrum. Other relics are the two snuffboxes containing the oldest snuff I have ever seen. Not that I have ever seen any new snuff. The only senator who uses the blotting sand provided on the desks is Senator Welker. He does it just to be ornery. Other traditional points of interest not shown to the general public are Daniel Webster's desk, in which he wrote his name, and the desk of Jefferson Davis, through which a Union soldier thrust his sword.

A miraculous transformation has taken place. Overnight I have changed from a rock-ribbed Republican no-dealer into a Democrat as solid as the South. I no longer associate with the greedy capitalists who champion Big Business and am a stalwart defender of the Little Man. I should amend that statement to read, "the Little White Man." Bobby Baker had for some time been horrified at the thought of subjecting me to the torture of having to be a Republican, and when Senator Smith brought up a page (male) I was transferred to the Democratic side. The only drawback is that we have to work harder on the Democratic side.

Today has been particularly zany for some reason. I suppose it is part of the relief everyone feels at getting rid of the gas bill. We are now considering the sugar bill, which is an effort to make everyone happy—the domestic producer and producers in Peru, Cuba, Mexico and so forth. Most of the debate was not overwhelmingly interesting, as the various senators were arguing for an increase of from 4 percent to 5 percent for somebody or other. All sorts of strange things happened. First, Senator Welker tripped and fell over a couch in the cloakroom while racing to the floor for a voice vote. He collapsed in helpless laughter on the couch. Then Senator Fulbright tried to railroad through a ridiculous amendment to the bill, which would have liquidated the domestic producers by removing their protection. It of course seems a good idea to me, a staunch free-trader. But everyone else seems to consider sugar an essential industry and spoke feelingly on the subject. The whole matter seemed so silly that only a voice vote was thought necessary to settle it. Fulbright and a couple of others shouted "Aye" so loudly that the chamber shook, and the overwhelming majority of opponents were unable to muster as much sound. So the chair announced that the amendment had carried. Everyone started laughing. Laughing hardest was Senator Fulbright. The matter was finally settled by having the various sides stand in their seats. When the three or four senators supporting the measure stood up, the laughter started all over again. The chair complimented them for being a loud minority. Then, to keep things going at a lively pace, one of the pages fell asleep and rolled off the steps full-length onto the Senate floor.

I was walking around town when I came across President Lincoln perched atop a bundle of fasces in front of a building labeled "Selective Service." I hurried past, pulling up my collar and looking in the opposite direction.

Washington was reeling today under the most nearly fatal blow since the War of 1812. The militant marching wing of the Women's Christian Temperance Union was here in fine intemperate mettle and never let it be said that the Capitol was blissfully unaware of the fact. The occasion was a public hearing before the Interstate Commerce Committee on the Langer bill, which proposes to ban television and radio advertising of that unpretentious beverage that Stephen Crane refers to as "beeh." I was first attracted to the hearing in the caucus room by the overflowing crowd trying to jam into it. The place was swarming with old ladies, their faces lit with indomitable self-assurance born of long-standing self-righteousness. They had come along to breathe in the healthful testimony in favor of the bill. And they had dragged along with them throngs of children to be enlightened. Of course the children of such strong-minded women were absolute terrors, and the generally stout-hearted elevator operators were pleading for mercy. There was some very touching testimony about how corrupting the sight of beer on television was to the tender impressionable minds of the young. Personally I think much too much has been made of innocent impressionable youth being led astray by violence as portrayed on television and in comic books. I also think there would be a lot of bankrupt stations if this bill were passed.

Senator Knowland, acting on the supposition that token opposition is better than no opposition and in order to demonstrate his unswerving dedication to the virtues of economy, has been systematically moving to reduce the appropriation for every committee. He finally acknowledged the futility of this opposition for the sake of opposition by saying that he was only introducing these motions to keep the record straight.

51

Today was one of those days when it is just fascinating to sit and watch the news as it rolls off the ticker. Also it is interesting to see the different editions of the papers as they are delivered to the Marble Room because each has a new screaming headline: "Gas Bill Vetoed." "U.S. To Send Tanks to Arabia." "U.S. Not To Send Tanks to Arabia." The only trouble is it is on just such days that you are never allowed to sit still. Every one of those headlines is intimately associated with the Senate. First, the news flashed over the wire that the product of over two solid weeks of prolonged debate had been voided: the President had vetoed the natural bas bill. A few minutes later I rushed in with the President's message accompanying the veto. The reporters started shouting with glee and sliding down the banisters in their hurry to get downstairs to record political reactions. The headlines about the tanks resulted from a campaign by Senator Humphrey, whose exposure of the deal resulted in an order issued by the President at 3:00 A.M. halting the shipment and imposing a temporary ban on all arms shipments to the area. Senator Humphrey has a tendency to be slightly reckless and quick on the draw, but in this case a growling watchdog turned out to be a valuable asset.

One day one of the pages called back to the cloakroom from the Senate Office Building, as we are always supposed to do, to ask one of the cloakroom assistants if there was anything to be picked up over there to bring back to the Capitol. Senator Z. answered the phone. The page said, "Are there any S.O.B.s over there?" using the conventional abbreviation to refer to errands to be done at the Senate Office Building. Senator Z. said, "Yes, but they're all out on the floor."

February 22, 1956

I broadened my sphere of influence today to include the judicial branch. A very distinguished man appeared on the floor and was warmly greeted by Senators Clements and Morse and by Bobby Baker. He sat down in back to watch the proceedings. I asked Clements who he was, and he immediately shepherded me up to be introduced to Justice Minton of the Supreme Court from New Albany, Indiana, just across the river from Louisville. The Justice was wasting some time before the opening of the Court on Monday the 27th, and so I had a chance to talk with him for about ten minutes. He asked me about myself, and I told him some of the reasons I had come up here and what I liked about it and that I was thinking of possibly going to Yale next fall. He asked me why and I said in order to get as far away from my small-town background as possible and to have a variety of different experiences. He had taken a law degree at Yale in 1916, he said. He recalled what a change it was, with his Indiana background, to associate with people from a different stratum with big ideas about their futures.

I asked him how he would compare his life as a senator and his present life in the Supreme Court. It was a lucky gambit and brought out some very interesting thoughts. He said he had enjoyed tremendously his one term in the Senate, and he started reminiscing about his defeat in 1940. He was Assistant Majority Leader under Barkley at the time, and he said he probably spent more time on the floor than most senators and that if he had spent more time writing letters to constituents he might have been reelected. But, he said, Willkie was the national Republican candidate in 1940, and, as Indiana was his home state, a great effort was being made to swing it for the Republicans.

He said that he had had a great deal more freedom of choice and action in the Senate. It is impossible for one senator to be informed on all matters, and so a good senator becomes a specialist in some field in which he is particularly interested and does his important work on legislation in that field. This means that a senator can generally occupy himself with work of interest to him. And in the Senate the contacts, official and social, are very broad. He contrasted this situation with his life in the Supreme Court. There, he said, everyone must be an expert on every issue that comes before the Court, whether it is particularly interesting or important or not. The justices must sit through all testimony on all cases and very often, having no previous knowledge of the issue, must decide exclusively from arguments presented. And a justice may be required to write an opinion on a subject on which he is very ill informed. This depends upon assignments by the Chief Justice. He characterized his present work as much more exhaustive and demanding. He added that his contacts were much more limited, working as he does with a small group of men. He emphasized that these contacts were pleasant enough but that the atmosphere was "monastic." He assured me that he had no regrets and only fond memories of his shift from the Senate to his more exacting position.

Senator Clements seems pleased that Governor "Happy" Chandler changed the date of the Kentucky primary from August to May 29; it means that Happy will have just that much less time to build up a candidate in opposition. Also Clements feels that he will be freer from official duties earlier in the session than he will be in July. He also seems pleased with the support given him by various small weekly newspapers. He showed me a couple of editorials from such papers. He said that if we got enough of these it would be worth more than the support of the large city papers.

There has been an interesting series of events, which indicates that at least at present the McCarthy bark is worse than the McCarthy bite. Back when I was on the Republican side, he asked me to get a speaking stand for his desk. It then sat on his desk for a couple of hours before he was to speak. Senator Sparkman says he does this as a sort of psychological warfare. He was going to speak against the Subcommittee on Constitutional Rights of the Committee on the Judiciary, headed by Senator Hennings, on the occasion of the discussion of its appropriation for the coming year. He objected to the work of the committee in relation to the security program and thought that it had done the system grave harm; presumably he was going to fight to reduce the appropriation. But, as at that time the question was a supplementary appropriation to cover only one month, McCarthy decided to withhold his speech for the time being to allow the whole matter to be discussed more thoroughly later and served notice that he would make his attack in due course when the appropriation for the whole year was being considered. Then I removed the stand, as it had served its psychological purpose. Again today there was the stand, an ominous reminder to Chairman Hennings that he would have a fight on his hands. First Hennings outlined the accomplishments and plans of the committee for about an hour. Ten minutes before he was through I obtained the information for the presiding officer that McCarthy was planning to speak for approximately fifteen minutes. Then McCarthy stood up and for the second time withheld his statement, this time on the grounds of the statement by Hennings that he was almost through with his work on the security program. I somehow feel that the mere statement that an injustice was almost concluded would not several years ago have had the effect of so pacifying Senator McCarthy.

So the whole affair was a false alarm and had its amusing aspects. Hennings had brought along practically the whole committee staff to assist in his defense, and all the time there was that speaking stand saying plainly, "You just wait," in answer to every statement in support of the appropriation.

I am auditing a government course at the Capitol Page School and try to get up often enough to keep up with the class. I would not say I am actually learning something in this course, but it does review and organize the information I have picked up from various places. We work on the floor until between 6:00 and 8:00 P.M. generally. Afterward I have time only to write letters and go to an occasional movie. I am trying to keep up my French in the mornings. I am now reading a gripping story called "La Femme Docteur" in a pulp magazine. It is about a lady surgeon who stakes her whole career on the big operation. It is a French translation of an English story.

Today is Washington's Birthday. It is traditional for a senator to read the Farewell Address and then for the Senate to adjourn. Deference was paid to custom to the extent that the Address was read by Senator Humphrey, but the farm bill was too pressing to allow for adjournment. Humphrey said that he was going to make no attempt to put something into the Farewell Address about Secretary Benson. He was all light and happiness as the big occasion approached. He did as creditable a job of reading as could be asked of a person with such an unfortunate voice. A surprising number of senators, notably Lyndon Johnson, turned out for the reading. I think it was the first time I had ever heard the whole thing, and it was extremely interesting.

The farm bill was taken up today, with Chairman Ellender of

the Agriculture Committee making his formal presentation. The transcript of the committee hearings on the bill were laid on each senator's desk. There were eight parts, which amounted to a stack about eight inches high on each desk. Also each senator is introducing an amendment to give special treatment to some group in his state. At last count there were 34 amendments ready to be introduced. Eisenhower will be in a spot if a farm bill passes with high supports. If he sticks to his public commitments and vetoes the bill, he will be in for accusations of junking the farmers completely.

I mentioned earlier that what little interest there was in the Case matter at the outset seemed to be generally an amused interest; that the special committee was appointed in deference to the public furor created, and that the members of the committee were bored stiff with the whole affair. Since then the papers have dressed the trivial Case affair in sweeping significance. And great interest in our election laws has grown out of this incident. This interest has taken different forms. Neuberger introduced a bill to provide for Federal government financing of campaigns. Humphrey will introduce a modification of this idea. The plan of the Majority and Minority Leaders has only been hinted at. But the greatest interest has been in an investigating committee that would deal with matters more sweeping and intriguing than the Case case. Senators recall that an unknown by the name of Richard Nixon gained fame through work on such a committee and that Estes Kefauver became a national figure through his work on crime. Add to such an investigation, in which there are sure to be some unpleasant facts, a guaranteed press because of the play the papers have already given it, and you have a lot of senators looking with favor on serving on such a committee. So what the senators laughed at before the papers got hold of it eventually led to a full-scale committee, with a budget of $350,000, supposed to take up where the 4-man committee charged with investigating the Case case left off, and investigate the general problem of lobbying and campaign contributions. There was a lot of excitement here today just before the names of the members were to be announced. Senator George, who was presiding, had the list on

56

the desk in front of him. The press gallery is directly above the rostrum, and a score of reporters were leaning precariously over the railing in an attempt to read the list on the desk below. Unfortunately, no one had remembered to bring his binoculars, so the attempt was futile. Reporters, senators and pages were all laughing at their frustration. The committee members named were Gore (D., Tenn), McClellan (D., Ark.), Anderson (D., N.M.), Kennedy (D., Mass.), Bridges (R., N.H.), Thye (R., Minn.), Goldwater (R., Ariz.) Purtell (R., Conn.). They are eight of the sharpest senators available.

An indication of the importance with which the senators view this explosive and highly publicized investigation is the presence on the committee of Senators Gore and Goldwater. Gore resigned a highly important post on the Democratic Campaign Committee to serve on this committee, and Goldwater resigned his position as Chairman of the Republican Senatorial Campaign Committee. I think there might be some objection to Goldwater's presence on the committee, for it was he who introduced the bill to ban the use of union funds in elections. The fact that campaign heads from both parties resigned to assume seats on the committee indicates what role is anticipated for it in the coming elections.

February 24, 1956

A guard sneaked a couple of us into the prayer room today. It is reserved for senators and representatives. It is small and very lovely. In the center is a stained glass window that dwarfs the room; it portrays George Washington praying and has the names of all 48 states entwined in the decoration. Some foresighted artist has left spaces for a couple more states.

During the past couple of days the emphasis has been on foreign affairs. Things were led off yesterday with a speech by Senator McClellan, which the press was assured was to be a bombshell. He told of testimony before his Permanent Subcommittee on Investigations of the Government Operations Committee (the one McCarthy headed during the 83rd Congress). He attacked the removal from the embargo lists of many items vital to the defense of the Soviet Union, which our allies can now ship behind the Iron Curtain. He said that these precision machine tools are more deadly than shells because they can be used more than once. He said that the Congress was not given a list of classified items because it was secret. McClellan gave as an example a certain machine, the more efficient form of which can be shipped to Russia but the less efficient form of which cannot be shipped. Senator Russell said that our policy is evidently to ensure that Russia doesn't get any obsolete equipment. The chief aide of this subcommittee is Robert Kennedy, the brother of Senator Kennedy. They look just alike, though the Senator looks older. Both wear their hair in their faces.

This speech was made on the Senate floor. It was a little more difficult for me to wangle my way into the second event emphasizing foreign affairs. This was the appearance of Secretary of State Dulles and Under Secretary of State Herbert Hoover, Jr., before the Foreign Relations Committee. Fortunately it was a slow day on the floor (they ran out of speakers on the farm bill and had to adjourn), so I was able to spend most of the afternoon in the four-hour session. The caucus room was stuffed and squashed. A long line of people was waiting. One reporter pushed his way forward with his press card, only to be told that all press spots were also taken. A friend of mine who works for the committee fixed me up with something to deliver to the chief counsel of the committee, so I was able to walk right in. The entire committee was present, along with scores of senators who just came to sit in on the affair, not to mention their wives. Senator Saltonstall had to stand for a while.

The two officials had been called primarily in connection with the shipment of eighteen tanks to Arabia, but questioning wandered generally all over the map. The papers said that this was the roughest time Dulles has had before the committee, but it was the first time I had seen Dulles—the second time I had seen Hoover—so I was not in much of a position to judge that.

Hoover took full responsibility for the tank deal. The tanks had been paid for by November, a month before the Red shipment of arms to Egypt, and were being shipped under a proper export license. The temporary suspension was only to double-check that everything was in order. Dulles said that the tanks could not possibly be used against Israel because of transportation problems. Most of these preliminary questions had been directed at Mr. Hoover, and the committee was anxious to get back to the star witness; the questions strayed to more general topics. Senator Fulbright, in his charmingly droll manner, tried to establish that the Communists had gained ground in the past few years. "On the contrary," said Mr. Dulles, "the Communists have failed." He said that the policy of power, intolerance and violence practiced under Stalin for thirty years had been abandoned in the face of continued resistance from the free world. The Communists are now searching around for a new policy and in so doing are borrowing from our policies, diplomatic and economic. They are not fully entrenched in any long-range policy but are attempting to build one around economic development. And, said Dulles, if we cannot beat them in this field, we ought to be ashamed of ourselves. He concluded these remarks by stating again his belief that the Communists have suffered a great defeat in their previous policy. At this point the audience burst into applause. Senator Fulbright, looking over his glasses, said in a tone of deep-throated mockery, "We-ell this is a remarkable demonstration." He would not accept such a bouquet of roses and started asking specific questions. The one thing for which Dulles did not have an immediate answer was the recent Communist advance in the French elections. He smiled, and said, "well," a couple of times, then said this was "an interesting phenomenon" (laughter). He then explained that the legislature was not very important in France and that the continuing body of civil servants in the highly centralized administrative organization assured France of a stable government and a prosperous economy.

The rest of the afternoon was spent in a mostly futile attempt to clarify our arms policy in the Middle East. The most specific statement was in Dulles' prepared remarks at the beginning of the session: "As I have indicated on previous occasions, the United States does not exclude the possibility of arms sales to Arabia at a time when it will preserve the peace. We do not exclude the possibility of arms sales to the other Arab states under similar conditions." He refused to answer many questions. He did make the following statements: that the shipment was in the way of confirmation of the grant of a United States air base by Arabia; that because of transportation conditions the tanks sent to Arabia for training purposes could not be used against Israel (Senator Barkley raised the obvious point that, if the tanks are for training purposes, more tanks must be expected for the trained men to use, but he received no comment); that no nation beside Russia and the United States can aspire to secure its defenses against aggressors, that is, neither Arabia nor Israel would be safe even if we shipped them arms; that, therefore, other means must be sought to ease Arab-Israeli tensions through work with refugees and settlement of border disputes; and that more arms can be safely absorbed by the 32 million Arabs than by the 1.7 million Israelis. This last point seems to have rather lukewarm morality. It indicates our basic willingness to ship arms to either place if in the exciting game of cat and mouse the art of politics so dictates. In the absence of a statement of general policy, these remarks point up the fact that no basic decisions have been reached on the Middle East.

At this point, Morse and Humphrey started needling Dulles about giving arms to a country like Arabia. They were not deterred by Dulles' statement that the original agreements were made by Roosevelt. Morse suggested that the tanks might be used to suppress dissident groups in this absolute monarchy. He said that he probably would join such a group were he there. Humphrey deplored the fact that Jewish Americans cannot do business in Arabia. He said King Somebody-or-Other had said that he would sacrifice the lives of 10 million of his subjects to suppress Israel. Dulles pointed out that King Somebody-or-Other had control over only 7 million people and that we must not expect our allies to be exactly like us in every respect, that we must respect their customs just as they respect ours. He mentioned the fact that Arabia had prohibition. "Aha," said Humphrey, "but prohibition is adhered to in many parts of our own country."

"Did you say *adhered* to?" said Dulles (laughter).

Senator Knowland asked for a live quorum today before Senator Aiken's speech against rigid price supports, in an effort to muster Republican support behind the attack. Quorum calls can be divided into two parts. Theoretically two-thirds of the senators should be present for all debates. In practice, between fifteen and twenty are there during most sessions. Those come who are particularly interested in the legislation under discussion. But anyone can suggest that a quorum is not present, and, if the fact is demonstrated after calling the roll, the Sergeant-at-Arms must produce the proper two-thirds. Generally quorums are called to waste time, to allow for the next speaker to get to the floor and so forth, and they are withdrawn before they are completed. But sometimes there is a live quorum, which means that they will go all the way through with it, that the Senate will not proceed until two-thirds of its members show up even if the Sergeant-at-Arms has to drag them over. Calling live quorums is not one way to increase your popularity. But sometimes the leaders get peeved and call them in wholesale lots.

February 27, 1956

A wide-eyed page appeared on the floor today to report that there was a woman outside the chamber who looked just like Jane Russell. Well, the Senate will only tolerate the real thing, and sure enough it was the lady with the raven hair and 38-inch bust. Reactions were varied. One married law student who works as an elevator operator said that he would give her only a "B—," that she looked too much like a horse. Another, however, became enraptured and poetic, saying that there was something regal in her air, that she walked like a princess and that she had a devastatingly beautiful voice. Perhaps the most graphic indication is what

61

happened when a couple of us were walking out of the Senate Office Building after work. She was coming up the steps, charging along at the head of a long line of managers and press agents. My friend dropped his school books in surprise. "Well," said the manager, "look what you did to him." I, of course, remained calm.

Harley Kilgore, Senator from West Virginia, died today (Tuesday) at the age of 63. I had only seen him a couple of times and knew nothing about him, as he has been in the hospital since I came to the Democratic side. His death places in the chairmanship of the Judiciary Committee perhaps the Senate's most outspoken opponent of the Supreme Court decision on segregation, Senator Eastland of Mississippi. Eastland is an intriguing person. He has a very loose ambling gait and an alert manner, which gives him a boyish appearance despite his balding head.

February 29, 1956

The speech of President Gronchi of Italy before the joint session might have been a big story had not another President barged in and upset everything. At least superficially the reaction to Eisenhower's decision to run again has been primarily amused relief. Clements characterized it this way: "Now, boys, of course you realize that I'm not as healthy as I used to be and I can't really do very much and everyone else will do the work for me, but I feel fine and dandy and want to be President. Of course, you realize I'm too weak to run." The relief was because at last that lingering doubt has been dispelled, and Democrats and Republicans alike know what they are up against. The decision seemed clear enough from the scheduling of the news conference in the morning; if he had been going to announce that he was not going to run he would have done it late in the day so as not to disrupt the stock market. Yet, though all logic pointed to the second term decision, that final word was needed to touch off the anticipated reaction.

All the Democrats had steeled themselves for the blow long ago and had a good time poking fun at the beaming faces of their Republican friends. Even the Democrats were relieved to hear the final word, so that they could swing into action with the knowledge that their attacks were not premature. The Secretary for the Minority slapped the Democratic Secretary of the Senate on the back and called out "How's your health?" He smiled back. Everyone could agree that knowing was better than not knowing, however unpleasant the knowledge might be.

As I wrote on the day of Senator Kilgore's death an unusual situation had been created in which Senator Eastland is in line for the chairmanship of the Judiciary Committee, which has the largest budget of any committee, handles more bills than any other Senate committee and, among other things, passes on nominations to the Supreme Court. Wayne Morse has undertaken to block his election (a simple majority in the Senate is needed) on the grounds that the Senator's public statements have shown racial prejudice. He asked the Senator to disqualify himself on these grounds. Such an opportunity could not be passed over without a reminder to Morse by Republicans that, had he remained true to the faith, the Republicans could be in control and leading the committees and the Senate would not be in such an unfortunate position in the first place. The reminder was made in a kindly spirit, a spirit mollified and uplifted by fond thoughts of November. Morse replied that often in life we must choose "among evils." That effectively silenced the Republicans.

Senator Stennis, the other senator from Mississippi, made a fiery defense of his colleague Eastland's personal qualities. Here we had a clash between the legal view of Morse and the personal view of Stennis. (I note in passing that, while all this was going on, Eastland himself was in the Marble Room calmly reading a newspaper.) Then Alben Barkley got up and made a very statesmanlike short speech. He said that ours was not a government of laws, nor was it a government of men, but a government of laws and men. That our preoccupation with one of these facets must not blind us to the other. It was a very diplomatic slap in the face of Mr. Morse. He mentioned that the seniority system has been in effect for 175 years and that it has been set aside in only three separate instances; that the whole system was given thorough study under the Legislative Reorganization Act of 1946, and that

63

the study could not come up with a better system of choosing chairmen than the seniority system. He warned of the committees' becoming objects of campaigning and political rewards. So, he concluded, in a most diplomatic and indirect fashion, a narrow legalistic view of human beings and human convictions must not blind us to the fact that our government is made up of individuals charged with responsibility to carry out the laws and that the seniority system is the most dependable way of shaping individuals into workable government organization. I think the damage done in not giving Eastland his committee when he refused to relinquish it himself would have been greater than what may result from his chairmanship. It may be distinctly beneficial from the standpoint of efficiency. No one questions Eastland's ability. I understand some bills have been passed several times by the House without action by the Judiciary Committee because Kilgore left something to be desired in the way of management. And if Eastland had relinquished the committee, Kefauver would have become chairman and then nothing at all would have been accomplished because the latter does not pay a great deal of attention to his senatorial duties, at least at present.

March 10, 1956

The announcement was made today that Senator McClellan has been chosen chairman of the Select Committee to investigate elections and lobbying. Senator Gore, the one designated by Johnson unofficially to be chairman, ended two weeks of controversy by withdrawing his name from consideration for the chairmanship. As it went without saying that a Democrat should head the committee, Democrats being in the majority, the logical choice was Gore. The trouble was that the choice was a little too logical. Gore was a little too well acquainted with the situation through his place on the Democratic Campaign Committee and as Chairman of the Subcommittee on Privileges and Elections. He is an acknowledged master of campaign strategy and more noted for his brilliance than for his impartiality. The Republicans were wary of such a person's having control of an investigation that could have a direct bearing on the November elections and counterattacked by attaching strict conditions to any chairmanship by Gore. There was no fear about the impartiality of Senator McClellan of Arkansas, presently Chairman of the Permanent Subcommittee on Investigations, which was McCarthy's committee during the 83rd Congress. I would say that he is positively the most unsensational senator available. He has filled the investigation post with perseverance and thoroughness and has accomplished much more than McCarthy, one reason being that he has deliberately sought to avoid publicity. While Gore impresses you with his shrewdness, McClellan impresses you with his dogged honesty. The Republicans realized that they were much less on the defensive under his leadership and quickly agreed to rules. His election is definitely a step toward accomplishing something constructive.

Well, at this point (Saturday), the preliminary debate on the farm bill is over, and the wrangling that goes with amendment and final passage is now in progress. It is a good time to review the various arguments in generalities, steering clear of the technicalities now being tossed around. The only conclusion to be reached from the discussion of the farm bill to which I have been subjected since February 22nd is that there cannot even conceivably be anything resembling a coherent farm program or a consistent farm policy, primarily because there is nothing coherent or consistent about the farm economy. The old saying that you can prove anything by the Bible goes also for the farm economy. It is possible to establish anything incontrovertibly, depending upon the examples and the reasoning you happen to choose. Senator Anderson, Democrat from New Mexico and Secretary of Agriculture under Truman, favors flexible price supports. He says it is only common sense when you want to stimulate production to raise the price and when you wish to curtail production because of a surplus to lower the price. This theory is proved conclusively by the trend in the flax and potato industries. Senator Ellender, Democrat of Louisiana, Chairman of the Agriculture Committee; Senator Morse, a man strong on principle if shortsighted in other respects, and Senator Humphrey, who has to get in a word or two

65

on every conceivable subject, all favor high rigid supports. They argue that it is only common sense that when a farmer's price is cut he will plant more crops to compensate for the lower unit intake. This theory is proved conclusively by the trend in the rice industry.

So there you have two very distinguished groups irreconcilably opposed after vast experience with the farm problem. The one common denominator that kept the bill from complete annihilation was the soil-bank plan, under which farmers are paid to take land out of production. It is the first constructive suggestion that has been put forward for the long-range settlement of the farm problem. The fact that it is truly worthwhile is attested by the squabble now going on between various groups claiming credit for the proposal.

The speeches have been fairly interesting. Senator Anderson is a distinguished person, who has quite a following among senators when it comes to farm legislation. He gave a fine speech, proving, as I said, that flexibility was the thing because of what happened in flax. Senator Ellender is one of those exasperating people who are workmanlike and intelligent but who just cannot make themselves understood. He evidently assumes that everyone has the vast grasp of the farm problem that he has. Senator Humphrey delivered a 350-page speech. They ran some of the sessions until 11:00 P.M. trying to get rid of the thing. The speech itself would not have been so bad if he had not gotten so inspired by reading his own words that he had to extemporize for five minutes at the end of every page. Senator Z. carried off the prize for the most colorful expression: "The farm problem has been on the lips of most of our tongues for some time." Senator Morse carried off the prize for the most uncompromisingly violent attack. It has been commented that it is hard to tell when Morse says something important because he gets too worked up about everything. This speech was described in the press as "slashing." He can work himself into a towering anger faster than any senator around. He is an extremely effective speaker, but he leads you to distrust the relative significance of what he is saying by spewing out his wrath about everything under the sun.

I was walking by the old Supreme Court chamber the other day and was amazed by the gorgeous if incongruous decorations. Blended together were palm fronds of tremendous size and beauty and a massive collection of red carnations. "Aha," said I, "this has all the earmarks of the party of special privilege." The tourists gave me a strange look and passed quietly by. It turned out that I was right. The decorations were straight from the botanical gardens to grace a meeting of Republican Women. Giving the ladies a rousing address, which had a sort of weak-kneed quality, as each syllable had to fight its way through impressive layers of blubber, was Senator F., who has been feverishly praying for another Eisenhower candidacy. His weak mind is just strong enough to realize he doesn't have a chance for re-election without Eisenhower. It is not strong enough to realize, however, that he doesn't have a chance with Eisenhower either.

I have been interested in following the reporting of perhaps the most newsworthy event I have witnessed, the appearance of Secretary Dulles before the Foreign Relations Committee to explain his actions in relation to the tank shipment to Arabia and the general policy of the State Department toward the Middle East. In some papers this appearance was described as the roughest time Dulles has had with Congress since he became Secretary. It was reported that many times he was flustered, "flushed and angry." Emphasis was placed upon the "sharply critical" attitude of the Democratic senators and the issue taken with his happy statements about free-world gains over the past couple of years. In *Time*, on the other hand, a very different picture was presented. There the emphasis was on the answers Dulles made to his critics, and his replies were printed without the comebacks from the Democrats. This treatment gave the impression that Dulles was answering Democrats with a bold confidence that left them speechless.

The other day Senator Capehart, the Indiana Republican, accused Humphrey of inconsistency in his stand on the farm bill. Humphrey retorted that he didn't think much of Capehart's record of consistency either and he wished to retain the right to choose his own professor. All the Democrats laughed; all that is except Estes Kefauver, in town for the farm vote, who does not feel greatly appreciative of Mr. Humphrey, who is doing everything he can to win Minnesota for Stevenson.

Something is very definitely in the works on the issue of segregation among the Southern senators. For some days now, small groups have been conferring in Johnson's office, poring over documents in the cloakroom and modifying and signing them in a very secretive manner. It is understood that the result will be a Southern ultimatum against the Supreme Court's desegregation decision. Modifications are being made, however, to make it palatable to more senators who are not outspoken on the subject—men like Daniel of Texas and George of Georgia. George stays out of such controversy as much as possible, but this stand is seen as indispensable for him, as he is up for re-election against Talmadge this year.

When Lyndon Johnson left town a couple of weeks ago, he was confident of a victory for 90 percent price supports by a comfortable margin of about eight votes. He confided that with this big a margin the chances of a Presidential veto were about even. He believed that, if the margin were closer, the President would in all probability veto the bill. What happened to Johnson's margin in the couple of weeks that he was absent from the Capitol resting up in Texas? The President was busy calling senators on the morning of the controversial vote. I know, for instance, of his call to Senator Russell. I doubt, however, that Eisenhower swung any votes. Republicans were already committed one way or the other, and Democrats had no particular desire to oblige. What seems to have been the major reason for the swing by around ten senators on the Democratic side (the margin of victory) to support flexible supports is the stand of Senator Anderson. Such a man's support for flexibility seems to have had its effect on borderline senators. No effort at persuasion is used on senators who have already made public commitments or who must vote a certain way because of pressures back home. The pressure is applied on, and the final outcome of the vote rests with, the senators with no public commitments from states not greatly affected by the pending legislation, who are thus free to vote their convictions and to change those convictions. Two examples of borderline senators are Alan Bible of Nevada and John Kennedy of Massachusetts. Neither is particularly interested in farm problems in general, and neither comes from a state that is vitally affected by the outcome of the vote. Both these Democrats voted for flexibility, which is one reason for the vote this afternoon of 54–41 (95 senators since Kilgore's death) in favor of Benson's flexible program. The importance of this vote is indicated by the presence of Senator Millikin of Colorado. It is the first time this session that he has voted. He has been near death for months and was wheeled in today only long enough to wheeze out his vote. This, therefore, was the first 100 percent vote of the session.

With the disposition of this controversial and well-publicized issue began the interminable wrangling over the other 93 amendments (less Anderson's one to cut rigid supports), which various senators had introduced to further the interests of groups in their states. After the first 22 hours of debate, six amendments had been disposed of. On Thursday the Senate stayed in session for ten hours and sixteen minutes and was not even able to get rid of the second amendment, proposed by Senator Hickenlooper of Iowa, to raise the quota on corn production. When it became obvious that this amendment was headed for victory, opponents thought that they might salvage something by attaching a rider that would also give favored treatment to sorghum producers. It was offered in the form of an amendment to the amendment of Senator Hickenlooper. Then as the debate progressed this amendment to an amendment was amended to clarify the language.

Senator Olin Johnston of South Carolina came over to the pages and in a very serious way said, "Why don't we include peaches in this amendment too?" By this time even the pages were confused, and a suggestion was made to recess until the next day to clear up the confusion that existed concerning the effects of these various provisions. The next day the amendment was passed in a further modified version.

One senator complained that whichever way he voted on the

bill he would lose twenty thousand votes. The junior senator from one state asked his senior senator how he should vote on the sorghum amendment. The senior senator said to the junior senator that he should vote in favor of it because there were a certain number of sorghum growers in their state. Senators who rushed in just in time to be recorded on various votes had little idea of how to vote and generally voted as instructed by the people with whom they happened to be closely associated. Many votes were changed when the senators found out what the vote was about. One vote was announced as 46–45 in favor of high supports on millable wheat. A recapitulation was called for, under which arrangement no person who has not voted previously can vote. When, under this arrangement, the vote was announced as 45–45, the right of the Vice-President to vote was challenged because he had not voted on the previous occasion. This challenge started an hour of heated controversy on the parliamentary question. In the end it was held that the Vice-President could vote at any time that there was a tie.

March 12, 1956

Henry Ford II testified today before the Subcommittee on Automotive Marketing Practices. Mr. Ford, young and confident, backed by a corps of officious subordinates, read a preliminary statement describing the gloriously amicable and mutually beneficial relationship existing between Ford dealers and management. He happened to mention, however, that one of Ford's officials is by chance a member of the Republican Finance Committee and in that capacity solicited a "substantial" amount of money from Ford dealers. This role was, of course, purely within his rights as a private citizen.

Senator Monroney seemed doubtful that the dealers realized that he was acting as a purely private citizen and asked whether the dealers might possibly have felt a slight pressure to contribute. This question led to a first-class debate, with everyone on the committee expressing his opinion on the relative evil of the situation.

Republican Potter said that it was no worse than a worker's being pressured by the union. Senator Payne said it was just like soliciting for the Community Chest. Mr. Ford just sat back and listened.

A row was started today by the introduction by Senator George (chosen because of his prestige) of the manifesto of nineteen Southern senators on the 1954 desegregation decision of the Supreme Court. They characterized the decision as an "unwarranted" use of "naked power." This move has been the first designed to unite and coordinate the various mutinous voices raised in objection to the decision. And it has forced a stand by many senators who would prefer to remain on the sidelines. Such a senator is Walter George. He has no desire to get into a brawl over the matter. He must, as Chairman of the Foreign Relations Committee, realize the effect of such a move on our dealings with foreign countries justly critical of our racial discrimination, so he has made no public declaration on this issue. Yet he also realized that removing himself from such a concerted drive would seal forever any chances that he might have for re-election to the Senate this fall. This has been one result of the united effort. Another surprise was the adherence of Senator Fulbright, a senator for whom I have great respect. He is from Arkansas.

The minutemen were immediately alerted and ready for the counterassault, spearheaded by those perennial soreheads, Morse and Humphrey. Humphrey started talking about bringing out a manifesto on the other side. The disagreement on the floor today was entirely among the Democrats, with not a Republican opening his mouth. The Democrats let no regard for charity or party line stand in their way as the most prolonged and animated discussion of the year took place. There have been previous sporadic denunciations of particular actions but no such general gathering of adversaries in large numbers.

A lot of tempers flared today as one of the biggest deals of the farm bill fell through. Senator Russell introduced an amendment to raise support prices on cotton. It was to be supported by all the Southern senators, and Senator Eastland was confident that, in return for his vote for flexible supports on the basic commodities,

71

Republican Aiken would lead his considerable faction of Republicans into the ranks behind this amendment. Eastland said in the cloakroom that Aiken was going to support the amendment.

Then, minutes later on the floor, Mississippian Eastland took a public stand against the amendment and the higher prices for his own cotton growers and debated with Georgian Russell on its merits, arguing that to survive cotton must lower its prices to levels competitive with synthetic fibers. Something had happened in those few minutes that convinced Eastland that the Republicans had backed out of the bargain and were going to leave him holding the bag (with the amendment inside), and so he also switched and voted against higher prices for his cotton growers. As it turned out the Republicans had backed out, and the amendment was defeated by a disgraceful margin. About that time tempers were really hot. No one was so undiplomatic as to question the integrity of Senator Eastland, but his colleague from Mississippi, Senator Stennis, referred to Republican Aiken as "Judas."

Asked by Senator Green how he thought the bungled, jumbled farm bill was progressing, Senator Humphrey replied, "It's hell."

The general story of what has happened to the bill is that all high rigid supports were voted out of the bill to begin with and now they are being put back in commodity by commodity. Twenty-one of the 105 amendments proposed have been adopted so far, with around sixty to go.

Senator Barkley told what must have been a very funny story about some senators and some young ladies on a fishing trip. There was something in it about running through the weeds, but the weeds were unidentified, and the cause of the running was missed by my informant. Stuart Symington was immensely amused. Significantly or coincidentally, the day after Senator Barkley told his fish story, I carried over for Senator R. some rather large fish (hygienically wrapped, fortunately) from his office to the Senate refrigerator.

William R. Laird III, Harley Kilgore's replacement from West Virginia, arrived and was sworn in on Thursday, and it must have been quite a thrill to him that on his very first vote he cast the deciding vote 45–44. He is 38 and very good-looking. He had a rough first day, for the Senate stayed in until 11:00 P.M. trying to finish the farm bill. He looked pretty exhausted after his first round of orientation, after more than ninety senators had introduced themselves and he had muddled his way through a rigorous day of routine. It was clear on Friday that Senator Laird was a freshman senator. He voted his convictions and voted in favor of an administration-tainted amendment to the farm bill. His senior colleague hastened to inform him that this might lead to criticism at home, and Bobby Baker said in instructing him how to change his vote, "I'll try to keep you from going astray." Laird laughed and, with some hesitancy about procedure, changed his vote. He is catching on rapidly.

Senators Kerr and Monroney of Oklahoma introduced an amendment that would have allowed cattle raisers to be included in the soil-bank plan, under which farmers are paid to take land out of production. Under the amendment the farmer would be paid for a certain number of cows per acre. The amount of ground equal to one cow is something called an "animal unit." This proposal created a lot of talk, everyone asking who was to decide just how many cows constituted an acre. The objection raised was that this would help only the big farmers who own their grazing land but not those raisers who lease government land. Thus Aiken called it a "millionaire's amendment," which was a slap in the face of sponsor Kerr, who is immensely weathy.

I spent the evening of March 13, after the New Hampshire primary in which Kefauver won a sweeping victory, at Kefauver's national campaign headquarters, located in a beautiful suite of rooms in the Pennsylvania Building. I went along with an industrious elevator operator under the Senator's patronage who spends a good many evenings there folding and stapling propaganda as a labor of love.

For the first hour or so everything was quiet and subdued. Someone in the corner was opening a parcel containing eight-foot portraits of the Senator's head. "I think they're left over from '52," said my friend. I was stapling together a four-page list of scandalous statements made by Secretary of Agriculture Benson. A tray

73

of glasses, earmarked for the victory celebration, was resting unobtrusively in a corner. No one looked in that direction.

When the first returns came over the ticker, everyone stampeded for the machine. Early returns were gratifying, at least to these rabid Kefauverites: Eisenhower 254 votes, Kefauver 27, Stevenson 7. "He's leading by almost four to one," observed one analyst.

The mood began to relax a bit. Soon what was taken to be a trend was noticed; it gave Kefauver without dispute seven of the twelve delegates, with five undecided. Pictures were taken, with Mrs. Kefauver (Estes was in Minnesota) reading the results with Jiggs Donohue, the campaign manager. Mrs. Kefauver, a redhead with circles under her eyes, but still very perky, felt sufficiently spirited to make the rounds and be introduced to all the faithful slaving away for Estes. I said we at the Senate wished that we could see more of the Senator. She said she wished that she could see more of him too. She seemed to bear up under the burden of his absence without too much strain by planning for the big move to Pennsylvania Avenue.

An imposing lady came over to offer me some advice on politics from her vast store of wisdom, collected from many campaigns. She said that she had started out just as I was, stapling releases, and intimated that I might go far. I asked her how successful her record of picking winners had been. "Well, I was working in Russell's campaign in '52. Of course I knew that he couldn't win and I was only doing it as a favor for Senator Ed Johnson. But this year I'm betting on the right horse." We helped deduce for her the reasons for Russell's defeat, and she seemed very pleased with the result. Then she struck out on a mission to get the latest dope and has not been seen since.

The Prime Minister of Ireland, John Costello, arrived for a Senate speech two days before St. Patrick's Day, and the Irish embassy sent down a box of green carnations for all the senators. The Democratic Campaign Committee (which, since Senator Gore's resignation to serve on the Select Committee, has been under the leadership of Senator Barkley) provided everyone with green donkeys for their lapels, designed to further a more Democratic celebration of St. Patrick's Day. A large model of this donkey was presented to the Prime Minister, who posed for pictures with it. The American Ambassador to Ireland—Bill Taft, son of the late Robert Taft—refused to pose with the donkey. When the Prime Minister entered the chamber, he was greeted by warm applause and the sight of a green carnation on the lapel of each senator. This reception must not have gone unnoticed, but Mr. Costello (accent on the first syllable) seemed scared stiff. He braced himself against the rostrum all through his prepared speech. He is small, has white hair and a timid appearance and was too scared to demonstrate much personality.

The speech was highlighted by the presentation to the Library of Congress of some letters written by an Irishman serving in the British army in the Revolutionary War who sympathized with the revolutionaries.

It is noteworthy that just preceding Mr. Costello's remarks to the effect that this is the greatest and most august deliberative body in the world, Senator Y. was speaking on a most asinine amendment he had introduced to the farm bill. It has been remarked that this fine man might be half decent if he were not always besotted. Senator MacNamara once said in a tone of genuine wonder, "He always looks drunk. He's not, is he?"

March 19, 1956

Estes Kefauver arrived in town today, weary and flustered, the day before the Minnesota primary, in order to vote for high supports on the farm bill, which was finally passed on Monday night at 10.30. Incidentally, Drew Pearson is all wet when he reports that holding the vote on the eve of the big Kefauver test was all part of a conspiracy on the part of Lyndon Johnson and Hubert H. Humphrey. Kefauver didn't even have time to go home; he dropped his bags and rumpled suit at the Senate door and asked me to take them over to his office in the Senate Office Building so that his staff might get his suit pressed. Among his other possessions were a *Life* magazine rumpled out of recognizable condition and an impressive folder labeled "Minnesota Speeches." It was a tiring day for the overworked Senator. He left his coat in the cloakroom and then completely forgot about it and where he had left it.

The farm bill was passed 93–2. Not a single senator was pleased with the bill in its entirety, and everyone expressed a pious hope that something miraculous might be accomplished in the forthcoming conference between House and Senate to iron out the differences between the two bills. In the Senate high rigid supports on all commodities were struck from the Committee bill and then put in commodity by commodity in disguised form. The soil-bank plan, under which farmers are paid the equivalent of their net incomes on certain acres for taking those acres out of production to alleviate the surplus, was strengthened by an amendment making cooperation by farmers mandatory instead of voluntary as proposed by the Secretary and the Committee. The advisability of this move is undetermined, for the entire soil-bank plan is a massive experiment anyway.

Taken up after the farm bill was the general subject of the electoral-college system of electing the President, with several detailed alternative constitutional amendments up for discussion. One, proposed by Estes Kefauver and Price Daniel of Texas, would split the electoral vote now held by each state into thousandths in proportion to the actual vote cast for the top three contenders. A second proposal would be to use the congressional district rather than the state as the basis for each contest. There would be 435 separate contests, rather than 48, and the winner in a district would win all the electoral votes of that district. In other words these are two alternative systems for splitting the electoral vote of a state, which is now cast *en bloc* to the winning side, regardless of the winner's margin of victory. At first glance both these proposals seem more democratic than the present winner-take-all system. Both seem theoretically attractive and desirable. And so opposition to such beautiful proposals must be studied with care.

Each of these two proposals received so much criticism, which I will outline later, that it was realized that neither could pass. So someone came up with the brilliant idea of combining the two unsatisfactory proposals and giving the state an option to choose which plan it would use, hoping to gain adoption of the proposal by lumping the two supporting factions together. This combination of two dissimilar systems was called a "two-headed hydra," a "monstrous and hideous creation." It is argued that Congress, by adopting this proposal, would be admitting that it could not decide on anything. It would be shunning the decision and leaving it up to the states, which would be neglecting the Constitutional responsibility of Congress. Any alternative plan of this sort is automatically disqualified because each state would be at liberty to adopt the plan that was most advantageous to it and to shift from one to another as the parties in power changed. But let us assume that each plan is standing on its own merits and examine each separately.

The congressional-district plan is obviously no improvement whatever over the present system. It would be possible by gerrymandering to ensure the victory of a certain party. And the added incentive of influence in electing the President would encourage the development of such tactics. The presence of this plan among two alternatives would also invalidate the dual plan, because states would hurriedly adopt only this district plan; it would then be possible for them to rig the elections by arranging districts within the states.

The Daniel-Kefauver proportional plan and the arguments in favor of its adoption are much more attractive. This plan for splitting the electoral vote of a state into thousandths in proportion to the popular vote seems on the surface to come as close as practicable to an actual popular election, which seems so truly and essentially democratic. It is argued that it is unfair for millions of votes of the minority in a state like New York to go unrepresented in the Electoral College. It is further argued that Republican votes in the Solid South should not be considered futile by their casters and that the growth of second parties in presently one-party states would be encouraged if a voter felt that his minority group need not win the state in order to be represented in the Electoral College.

The opposition is led by John Kennedy, boy senator, war hero and Democrat from Massachusetts. He bases his opposition to the amendment on an overall view of our system of Constitutional government, rather than on an isolated discussion of the choice of the chief executive. He emphasized in reviewing this overall picture that the small states, the states in the South and the West, have a disproportionate influence in Congress and, because of antiquated districting methods, the urban areas are underrepresented within state legislatures. Thus, he said, after reviewing this inequity, any step that seeks to destroy another prerogative of the urban voter is a step away from popular election and true democracy. Then, turning to the problem at hand, he stated that the proportional plan would do the following:

1. It would increase the power of one-party states in the South and Midwest. In those states the vote is small (13 percent in Mississippi) and since congressional representation is based on total population, not on voting population, a much smaller vote controls an electoral vote in Mississippi than in Montana, where the vote is 73 percent. In Mississippi, an electoral vote represents 36,000 popular votes. In Illinois, an electoral vote represents 166,000 popular votes. Therefore, small unanimous votes in the South could, under the proposed system, outweigh much larger, much closer votes in other sections.

2. Also greatly increasing the power of the one-party states under the proposal would be the fact that the extremely large vote in urban areas of pivotal states, which is closely divided, would be virtually canceled out if the losing side were permitted its proportional share of the popular vote in electoral votes. Thus the large states, which are now so poorly represented in Congress, would also be deprived of any significance in the choosing of the President, and the power would rest in small one-party states where a candidate could pile up large electoral margins. The city voter would be disregarded, and the handouts and special privileges would be directed to the already pampered rural areas.

At present the outcome of the election depends to a great extent upon the results of state races in nine "pivotal" states with large populations, indeed with 51 percent of the nation's population. This is because these states shift from party to party, carrying with them large blocs of delegates. If this vote were to be split between the two parties on a proportional basis, the significance of a victory for either side would be trivial beside the large one-sided margins piled up in the South and in New England. Both sides in the argument agree that at present large states have a large share in the choosing of the President (Senator Daniel points out that 16 of 26 recent major-party candidates have come from those nine states) and that much of this importance would be lost under the proposed plan. Senator Daniel considers it unfair that a Republican vote in Alabama is less important than a Republican vote in New York. Senator Kennedy argued that any influence the large states may have is not nearly what they deserve and pointed out that urban areas are underrepresented in Congress and that it takes many more votes in a two-party state to win an electoral vote than it does in the apathetic South.

3. As even a small percentage of the popular vote would be reflected in the electoral vote if it were divided into thousandths, the third-party incentive would be greatly increased. Under our present system the third-party threat is virtually nonexistent because of the necessity of winning a majority in a state before any recognition whatever is given in the Electoral College. If official recognition were hung tantalizingly before third-party groups, much more splintering and factionalism would result.

The clinching argument of Senator Kennedy, however, was the most practical one. He pointed out that only one miscarriage has occurred in the 175 years in which we have been using the present system—and that under the proportional plan that gives small unanimous votes power over large close votes three minority presidents would have been elected. He proved that William Jennings Bryan would have been elected twice had this system been in effect at the time.

Senator Strom Thurmond, Dixiecrat candidate for President in 1948 and Democratic Senator from South Carolina, is one of the movers of the compromise "two-headed hydra" plan. I asked him whether or not he thought he had the necessary two-thirds majority. He said he did. I asked him his opinion as to whether or not the Congress was shirking its duty in giving the states two alternatives. He smiled and hedged on that one, saying that either plan would be an improvement on the present system. I remarked that at least there seemed to be unanimity of aim between the opponents and proponents of the measure, that in the end everyone is striving for direct popular vote and that it is only a disagreement over which system will come closer to it that is causing dispute. Thurmond, however, disagreed and said that he was opposed to direct popular election. He gave as his reason his belief that there should be 48 separate elections, not one national one, because Communist infiltration is more difficult if there are so many separate institutions. This is an argument in favor of state's rights I have not heard before. He has the most wonderful Southern accent in the Senate. It is phenomenal. He is also one of the most pleasant and considerate senators.

March 23, 1956

"Father has blessed the campaign. Isn't that nice of him? He's a Catholic but I guess his blessing is as good as anybody's." My lady friend, her eyes bleary with excitement, greeted me with this jovial promise of things to come when I first arrived on the scene this Tuesday evening to learn of the latest casualty reports from the Minnesota siege. My impression of the scene at Kefauver headquarters was one of unexplainable irrational unreality. There was a glowing ebullient lift in the air, which evidenced itself in the carefree way in which the cases of beer and cokes were being carted in. There was none of the averting of eyes and cautious steering of conversation that had characterized the early evening of the New Hampshire returns. It was certainly not because anyone suspected the tremendous margin by which Kefauver would eventually win. If anything tangible, it was the realization that Kefauver had nothing to lose and everything to gain that gave the gathering its spirit of elation and confident expectation. The first returns (Stevenson eight, Kefauver seven) were greeted with good humor, and there was no trace of the analytical anxiety that had been present on the previous Tuesday evening. Then the real trend began to show (Kefauver 59,000, Stevenson 43,000; Kefauver 107,000, Stevenson 72,000), and as each favorable return came in it was accepted with pleasure and no surprise. Everywhere there was a feeling of expectancy that was only fulfilled by the returns, and there was no shocked incredulity.

When the radio brought in an interview with Governor Freeman, who had vigorously backed Stevenson, and the Governor said, "Well, of course the returns are not exactly what we had hoped for," there was a general chorus of raucous laughs and gibes. Later, when the station canceled another trip to Stevenson headquarters because of "technical difficulties," there was another burst of amusement. One enterprising soul tried to compensate for the end of the beer by circulating a large box of Kefauver buttons. People vied to see who could squeeze on the most.

Kefauver had a rigorous schedule on Tuesday. In the afternoon, after introducing his amendment regarding the Electoral College here in Washington, he left for Minnesota, where he spent the evening listening to the returns. At 3:00 A.M. he left for Montana, and the next day it was California.

Senator McCarthy has been removing the drapes from the "new look" during the past couple of days. He has displayed a responsible outlook on life and has actually found something praiseworthy in the present administration. The start of the whole affair was an attack that Senator Neuberger, Democrat of Oregon, made on Secretary of the Interior McKay, who is to be Wayne Morse's opponent for his Senate seat this fall when Morse returns to the voters in his recently assumed Democratic role. The Neuberger attack itself was insignificant and not tremendously exciting. When McKay announced the appointment of one of the employees of the Interior Department as his campaign manager, Neuberger immediately took this as grounds for an assertion that he was mixing business and politics. He called for the man's immediate resignation from his post as counselor to an Indian tribe. He charged McKay with filling jobs at his command with old cronies.

It was surprising to see Joe McCarthy rising in defense of Secretary McKay because the Senator has few kind words to say about anyone or anything and does not go out of his way to be polite to the Eisenhower administration. It was easier to understand his scathing personal attack on Neuberger than his statement that McKay had been doing an "admirable" job. McCarthy squashed

Neuberger so flat it was funny. McCarthy took his heavy hand and slapped him so tellingly that Neuberger had a hard time reeling around the brink of confusion. With no forewarning about the attack on McKay, with no preparation on the subject, McCarthy squeezed contradiction after contradiction out of the flustered Neuberger. There was no artificial courtesy in his blank questions. "Please tell the Senate whether you realized you were in error when you stated that this man was paid out of tribal funds and whether you were deliberately trying to deceive the Senate." "The Senator has deliberately misread the law in stating that Secretary McKay appointed this man. It was done with the consent of the tribe involved." "I regret that the Senator did not know what he was talking about when he got up to make such a grave attack."

The McCarthy style, which is as refreshing as a slap in the face, was unchanged. His voice still retained its exciting ominous quality, its guttural menacing monotone. He was still unashamedly vicious and forthright in his unpleasantness. His unrelenting persistence while Neuberger tried to squeeze out from under the paw with which McCarthy was pinning him was that of a lion relishing the final blow to an insolent rabbit.

All these elements were unchanged. What had changed was the objective. There seemed apparent a certain party loyalty and respect for institutions that had been obscured in his previous absorption within himself. And though the pleasure of the chase was still apparent, there seemed to be a little more attention paid to the goals in question. He was seeking clarification of something that had no direct relevance to him and was working on behalf of someone who had been slandered.

Tuesday, March 27, 1956

Today the proposed "two-headed hydra" Constitutional amendment (under which each state would be allowed to choose which of two terrible proposals it would least object to) was defeated on a trial vote, 48–37, with a two-thirds majority necessary for passage. I have already discussed the two proposals. Under the Mundt plan, there would be a separate contest in each congressional district rather than in each state as at present. It would be unworkable because of the increased rigging of congressional districts by the state lesgislatures. Under the other alternative, the Daniel plan, the electoral vote of a state would be divided into thousandths in proportion to the popular vote cast for each candidate. This would mean the virtual annihilation of the influence of such states as New York and Illinois, for a victory in either state by a close margin would have much less significance than a one-sided margin in a one-party state. It would also be unfair because electoral votes are based on total population, not on voting population, and a much larger percentage of the people vote in the closely contested races than in the one-party elections.

The measure was not irrefutably defeated, but on a test amendment it was seen that the necessary vote could not be mustered, and before final action was taken the bill was sent back to committee. Bobby Baker has been trying to persuade Sanator Daniel that there are not sufficient senators in favor of the proposal. He took a confidential survey of the views of all Democratic senators, which showed that only five Republican votes would be needed to defeat the measure. And, after a test vote, this survey was borne out to the satisfaction of Senator Daniel. It was decided that the Senate floor was not the place to write Constitutional amendments, and instead of trying to come up with another compromise at the last minute he agreed that the whole matter should be sent back to committee.

If I had been in doubt as to which side to support in this fight, it would have been decided by the revelation (through their votes on an alternative proposal to implement direct popular election) that the people who were really for popular election opposed the "hydra-headed" amendment, while those who opposed popular election were in favor of it. This position on the part of the supporters of the Daniel-Kefauver-Mundt amendment completely voided their arguments that they were trying to get closer to the popular vote in their plan. Almost everyone (except Strom Thurmond) has been giving lip service to the idea that direct popular election of the President would be the best plan ideally. In presenting his proposal, each senator has shown how closely his system would correlate with the popular vote. Senator Daniel (among others) is thus contradicting himself when he calls it an evil that presidents are elected without a majority of the popular vote, says that his plan will correct this evil, and then opposes direct popular election.

It becomes more and more obvious as a debate of this sort progresses that no side has a monopoly of virtue. There are, I have to admit, some partially justifiable objections to the popular election of the President, beside the practical realization that such a proposal would never be adopted because there are enough small states receiving disproportionate benefits from the present system to block its adoption. Voting requirements, for instance, are at present left up to the states. Kentucky this past year voted to lower the voting age to eighteen. It had a perfect right to lower that age to one year if that was what Kentucky citizens wanted. It is argued that, if each vote were to count, such unjustifiable acts would occur as states attempted to increase their influence. Such attempts are now curtailed because each state is limited by a specific number of electoral votes, which it casts despite the size of the popular vote. If a scheme of direct popular election were adopted, so argues Senator Mundt, one state would lower its voting age to twelve because at twelve people are old enough to be Boy Scouts and therefore should be allowed to vote. Then another state would lower that age to eight because at eight you can be a Brownie, and, if you're old enough to be a Brownie, you're old enough to vote. In answer, Senator Pastore says that a state would not do that because it would simultaneously be changing the voting requirements for electing its governors and senators and thus would be "cutting its throat to spite its face."

State's righters also have reasonable objections to a popular vote for President. They think it would reduce the states to the status of mere accrediting agencies in a national election. That would mean Federal control of the national election, and Federal control of anything is to be eschewed right and left. The state's righters see beyond the present proposal to the next logical step, the Federal government setting up voter qualifications ensuring the right

84

of each citizen to vote. Thus the popular-election proposal appears to the South to be a neatly wrapped package with "civil liberties" stamped in big red letters all over it.

The Kennedy-Douglas forces have waged a very effective fight against adoption of the proposed amendments. It is almost unheard-of for the sponsor of a piece of legislation to withdraw his support. The compromise proposal bore the names of 54 senators, but after the Kennedy-Douglas barrage only 48 stalwarts were left championing the cause. Notables among the defectors were Ives of New York, Smith of New Jersey and Morse of Oregon.

Senator D. holds the distinction of following to the Senate someone who committed suicide. There is very little else to be said to the credit of the distinguished Senator, if indeed that is to his credit. This reflection is stimulated by his performance on the floor this afternoon, Wednesday, when he wasted well over an hour pleading for the adoption of a bill to which there is no opposition.

Senator D. is one of those people who think they are of tremendous importance to humanity and that every pungent syllable that falls from their lips is of urgent and critical importance to the salvation of mankind. On both counts he is in error. Senator D. struts. No other word can effectively describe his stuffy pompous gait. He invariably begins a speech by saying in his affectedly impressive voice, "I am not accustomed to speaking to empty desks," as he glances around the hastily vacated chamber. He invariably and unfortunately does accustom himself, however, to the extent of several hours. He spends a great deal of time expressing shock at the legislation presented by his colleagues and very little time attempting to do anything about it. When Senator Neely referred to the Senate as the "cavern of the winds," perhaps he was thinking of Senator D. When Senator Neely said, "It has taken the Senate three times as long and twice as many words to debate the farm bill as it took the Good Lord to create the world and all the windbags that dwell therein," he was thinking of Senator D. The good Senator D. himself was too busy gesturing and posturing to catch the reference.

On Easter morning at 7:00 A.M. I went to hear Billy Graham preach. So did thirty thousand other people. It is a little difficult to understand why thirty thousand people wrench themselves free from their radios long enough to shiver for an hour on wet ground. I suppose it is related to the Hindu concept of darshan, signifying a certain type of religious experience to be gained from associating with several million people around the feet of a great man. Roy Rogers and Dale Evans sang a jazzed-up version of "The Old Rugged Cross." Billy Graham gave a vigorous speech, which boiled down to the statement that Christ is the answer to everything; he didn't expand on that. According to the paper we were "electrified." One of the things to which Christ is the answer is the international situation. As an example of this, Graham told a story of how a certain delegate to the United Nations voted against France on an important international issue simply because the French delegate forgot to speak to him that morning. Although it may be an oversimplification, the story brought to mind an example of how important personalities and trivialities may become in deciding consequential issues.

Clinton P. Anderson, Democrat from New Mexico, is former Secretary of Agriculture and probably knows more about agriculture than any other person in the Senate. He has served on the Agriculture Committee with distinction and has had much to contribute. He has worked with conscience on every issue confronting the Committee, and any faint insinuation of partisanship on his part would simply fall flat on its face. His conscience has led him to desert his party on many occasions, and during the recent farm debate he continually spoke out for the administration. This man can render invaluable service to farmers because his knowledge gives him a large following among senators; and in his position on the Agriculture Committee he was well placed to render that service. Yet one of the unpublicized results of the farm debate was the resignation of Senator Anderson from the Committee. It will have far-reaching effects and will work to the detriment of the farm economy of this country. And the cause of this blow to millions of people was a petty personal squabble.

The debate on the farm bill was at many points heated and often unpleasantly so. As the administration met defeat after defeat, Senator F., an administration spokesman, felt the pressure mounting on him. He began to make irrational statements. As Senator Humphrey said, "He can call me a dirty bastard, but I'll be darned if I'll let him call me a murderer." This happened during the discussion of the school milk program. He made sweeping accusations about the political motives of the "Democrats." This did not sit well with the tired Anderson, who had time after time fought off heavy pressure from within his own party to vote with the administration. And so from frayed nerves and rash statements grew the conviction on the part of Senator Anderson that he could not work any longer with Senator F. and that he had to resign from the Committee. When Senator F. realized what he had done, he tried to apologize, but Anderson had made up his mind. All of this may seem a little far from the subject, but to me it brought home Mr. Graham's point.

Overheard, one senator to another, "Well, even if you don't believe it, you have to be sincere."

On Thursday night the various state societies of Washington, which choose the princesses to represent each state in the Cherry Blossom Festival, threw a ball at the Statler for the 53 princesses. Several of the pages got in as ushers, and after the program we were able to dance for the rest of the evening. It was pretty crowded, for each princess' dress took up enough room for five people. I danced with Miss Vermont, among others.

On the day of the festival parade the temperature was 85 degrees, it was a perfect night for the parade except for the fact that there was a tremendous wind blowing and the people carrying banners of various sorts were practically swept off their feet. Ocean Beach, Maryland, had a float with a beach umbrella and beach balls and so forth, and the lovely young ladies in bathing suits were having a dreadful time keeping everything on the float. Their umbrella soared away a couple of times, and someone was always happy to accommodate by rushing back with the beach ball when it scurried away. On the Guam float there were all sorts of lovely ladies lolling around a gentle little fountain, which suddenly started shooting water twenty feet into the air; it descended on everything, to the understandable chagrin of the young ladies.

April 12, 1956

Senator Jenner is a reactionary, but he is an absorbing reactionary. He gave a thrilling speech on why we should junk the farm program and particularly all contacts with foreign countries. "Our Government is like Penelope of Greek legend. Penelope knit by day and unraveled by night. That is what our Government is doing with the farm program. What little is knit by our agricultural officials is quickly unraveled in the stealth of the night through the State Department." An example of this foreign foolishness is sending United States technical assistants abroad to raise productivity of famished nations because this competes with artificially stimulated United States prices. Jenner always goes around with his head thrust forward in a gesture of intensity, pursing his lips in a grimace of fierce determination.

It is impossible to convey how droll Senator Dirksen sounds when delivering a speech in his precise oratorical style and in the most devastatingly beautiful voice imaginable. It rolls like the ocean; it undulates with the pathos of humanity. His big soulful eyes have all the heartrending quality of those of a discontented cow.

Nine-year-old Lucy Johnson,[2] daughter of the Majority Leader, was cavorting around in the Democratic cloakroom on the evening of the vote to approve the conference report on the farm bill, which restored the rigid 90 percent of parity. There was some talk about Mother Ladybird's attempts to keep candy out of her daughter, and various political remarks also slipped out. On the possi-

[2] She subsequently changed the spelling of her name to the more familiar "Luci."

bility of Kefauver getting the nomination: "Not if my father has anything to say about it." On the possibility of Johnson himself getting the nomination: "We love our daddy. We don't want him to be President and have another heart attack." Lyndon came into the cloakroom and found Lucy in the phone booth. She was talking to some chum. He dragged her out, saying: "I want you to meet a very important person who came in here just to meet you. This is the Vice-President, Alben Barkley." Cordialities were exchanged. Afterwards, Lucy said, "Aw shucks, and I was right in the middle of a nice conversation, too."

The only significant piece of legislation discussed during the past week was a proposal by Senator Mansfield of Montana to set up a supervisory joint committee of Congress, modeled after the Joint Committee on Atomic Energy, to supervise the activities of the Central Intelligence Agency. Senator Mansfield based his pleas on the fact that the President and the White House pretorian guard have during the past twenty years been arrogating congressional prerogatives, while the Congress has stepped limply aside. He feels that the Central Intelligence Agency is a prime example of this trend.

All the operations of the CIA, down to the salaries paid its officials, are cloaked in ominous and, for all we know, guilty silence. Senator McCarthy has one hundred pages of conclusive evidence of staggering graft, inefficiency and Communist infiltration that have completely incapacitated the agency, in his view. No one seemed dreadfully impressed with that, but McCarthy was hard to refute because no one really knew what the situation was. Through either congressional ineptness or executive adroitness officials of the CIA have appeared before the Armed Services Committee on only two occasions during the past year and before the Appropriations Committee only once, when they came to ask the benighted senators for a lump sum.

Senator Saltonstall was the administration spokesman and argued that after all ignorance has its blissful points, that there are certain things that it is not wise for him, as a senator, to know. This got Wayne Morse all riled up, if indeed anything in particular is necessary to bring him to a boil. He said that he had gotten sick and tired, as a member of the Armed Services Committee, of having army officers come before the Committee and, raising an Olympian eyebrow and glancing meaningfully at a shoulder covered with brass, state mystically that their achievements are beyond comprehension, more particularly the comprehension of the Senate. Morse conceded that it might be better for him not to know certain things, but he was damned if he was going to let someone else decide what he should and should not know, especially some brass-plated knucklehead.

Well, more powerful if not necessarily wiser heads prevailed, and Senators Russell and Hayden, Chairmen of Armed Services and Appropriations, had their way; the proposal was defeated. Russell said it was one of the disillusioning things about the Senate that it only took a couple of days for something reported in a closed session to get into the papers. It could be said, however, that Senator Mansfield accomplished his purpose of focusing attention on the lack of supervision of the CIA, and the Armed Services Committee will probably pay a little more attention to it in the future.

Attorney General Brownell testified the other day before the Immigration Subcommittee of the Committee on the Judiciary. Senator Eastland the Bold heads both committees. Also around was my favorite dullard, Senator Z. The Attorney General (he was addressed as "General" by the committee counsel) was present to review the progress of the Immigration Department of the Justice Department and to support certain legislative proposals to improve that service. As things have been so slow lately, I was able to hear him out through 33 pages.

He began with a general review of the progress that has been achieved during the past couple of years in the administration of the Department. He told how the Commissioner has reduced the problem of wetbacks from Mexico to one-thirtieth of what it was several years ago by centralizing and reorganizing the border police. He then proceeded to proposals for legislation. At present we have a system of quotas for each country based on a census taken in 1924. That census determined in a very rough and inadequate fashion the national origins of all the immigrants who then resided in this country, and quotas were assigned giving each country a proportion of the immigration quota corresponding to their proportion of the immigrant population in 1924. On the basis of this census, five-sixths of the immigration allotments go to northern Europe. Since economic patterns have changed, many countries do not fill their quotas each year, while in many others there are more applicants than there are places under the quota system. This inequitable system resulted in the situation last year in which only a little more than half the allotted 150,000 immigrants actually entered the country. Mr. Brownell proposed increasing the total quota figure by sixty thousand, to be assigned for the most part to those countries that are oversubscribed. He also asked for a system in which unused quotas could be assigned to other countries of the same continent. This would mean the traditionally undersubscribed quota for northern Europe would be assigned to traditionally oversubscribed southern and eastern Europe.

The Attorney General did not have affection showered upon him. The chief counsel asked him to admit that we would be altering our cultural pattern considerably by thus shifting the emphasis to eastern Europe and by allowing many more immigrants to enter the country. The "General" refused to subscribe to any such view. Fearless Senator Eastland sat crunched up in his chair, chewing his cigar in defiance, with his legs propped up against the table in front of him. Homely Senator Z. interrupted the General with a sage comment or two. He evidently isn't to blame for his idiotic expression and the fact that he talks like Mortimer Snerd. He is really a very nice chap and always gives me a wide, if blank, grin. Brownell himself is startlingly short, just as is Eisenhower himself on first sight. It might be an interesting project to discover the average height of the Cabinet to decide whether Eisenhower has an aversion to having people taller than he is around him.

On Tuesday I was an unwilling handmaiden to the most brazen little bit of political indiscretion I have yet witnessed. Commissioner Q. of the Federal Trade Commission is up for renomination this year. He evidently is a little apprehensive. On the day of the opening of the baseball season, with the Senate in recess to mark the occasion, he sent to several dozen strategically placed members of Congress, and several members of the Supreme Court as well, copies of a specially prepared *Daily News* with full-page headlines reading "Clark's Hit Wins for Senators" (sent to Justice Clark), "Hayden's Hit Wins for Senators" (to Senator Hayden) and so forth. On an inside page was a picture, labeled "Our Hero," of the back of a stout balding man, who could have been almost any senator, swinging at a ball.

I can testify to the origin and extent of the copies sent to senators, as I delivered many of them. According to newspaper reports, copies were also furnished to the Presidential party at the game, with headlines reading "Sherman Adams' Hit Wins for Senators."

The Commissioner's little joke did not go over big with Senator P., who was among the recipients of the *Daily News* story. All the papers that read "P.'s Hit Wins for Senators" were immediately burned. Senator P. had stated in his radio-television broadcast to his state on Tuesday night that the reason that he was not personally in the state to open his campaign for re-election was his pressing duties in Washington. He thus wants no revelation of the fact that he attended the opening game on Tuesday and was quick to burn anything that said "baseball."

Congress passed and sent to the President last week a farm bill that has been described, and described accurately, as "amorphous." The Presidential veto was the worst-kept secret since the President's decision to run again. Everyone sat around kidding and preparing his denunciation speech. Senator Fulbright said in his usual droll way, "The President was for the gas bill and he vetoed it; he's against the farm bill so he'll probably sign it."

Here are two samples from the denunciation speeches. Senator Ellender: "The President . . . has chosen to let our farm population dangle at the end of Secretary Benson's flexible noose. . . . It may be that he was too busily engaged in playing golf at Augusta to give our bill the study and consideration it obviously deserved." Senator Kerr, Democrat of Oklahoma, star debater on the Democratic side, who uses every single one of his 250 pounds for emphasis: "Mr. President, from his ivory tower at the Augusta Country Club, where he has been completely insulated from the voice of the people, the President has vetoed the Farm Bill passed by the Congress. With complete disregard of the economic depression and threatened bankruptcy of millions of farm families he has crucified them on the cross erected by Benson. . . ."

For the sake of argument, one might assume that the Democrats' high supports and the President's veto were arrived at on the basis of principle and honest deliberation. From this point on, however, no such polite estimate can even be advanced. The President and Benson have always argued, and the President reiterated in his veto message, that high price incentives are the chief cause of the surpluses that the President views as the root of all agricultural ills. Yet, on the same day that the President vetoed high price supports offered him by the Democrats, he himself, using the administrative power already at his disposal, raised the support prices of many products now in surplus, thus completely defeating any argument he might produce regarding parity principles. "A reason for setting the supports as we have is our feeling that farmers should not be penalized by the failure to get soil-bank legislation for this year's crop," said Secretary Benson before the Senate Agriculture Committee. This has a solicitous, if not downright political, ring to it.

On the Democratic side, blocking a measure that would include only the soil bank, which has been supported unanimously, would also be a clearly political move. This action by the Democrats seems all too imminent. Thus, following the President's veto message, we have two frankly political moves, one on the part of the Republicans, one on the part of the Democrats. They emphasize the fact that the President removed the farm bill from the realm of purely legislative deliberation, if indeed it ever was free from political maneuvering, and tossed it squarely into the middle of this year's political brawl. Politicians have been rushing in from all sides to fill the vacuum created by the veto.

I have been discussing the farm bill from a purely political

93

standpoint. Personally I am convinced that the President did the right thing because (1) Clinton Anderson, former Democratic Secretary of Agriculture favored flexible supports; (2) Truman's platform in 1948 promised them, so that Democratic gasps of chaste horror at the mention of the sliding scale seem rather ludicrous; (3) employees of the Senate Agriculture Committee favor flexible supports.

At the appearance of Benson before the Committee following the veto, he was in complete charge of the situation. Ellender, who was there, did not venture an attack in his presence, and another floor voicer of incredulity, Hubert Horatio Humphrey, did not even show up for the hearing.

Senator Ellender and the Agriculture Committee started hearings on the farm bill in April 1955. They spent months in the field, months framing the bill, a month on the Senate floor, several more weeks in conference with the House. The President, spending about 36 holes with the bill, completely nullified a year of work. So it was only natural that Ellender felt like letting off a little steam. He made some personal charges against the President on the floor and boasted that he would have Benson before his committee for an explanation. So Benson dutifully appeared on Thursday with the explanations. Ellender was considerably more subdued without the front-row cheering section of Fulbright, Kerr, Frear, *et al.*, to egg him on, and Benson emerged unscathed.

Benson is a very unexciting person. He has no distinguishing characteristics at all. He is fat, of normal height, balding, uninspiring in every respect. He was pleasant and confident and always had an answer ready.

It was significant that, while most of the members of the Committee have made spectacular critical speeches on Benson, in his presence almost no one made more than the polite statement that it just so happened that they were in disagreement with the Secretary's policies. The only attack attempted on the Secretary was by that endless source of my amusement, Senator Z. He made what he thought was a chiding political gibe. With an attempted sly grin, which ended up as a lopsided and idiotic smirk, he tried to insinuate that Benson was supporting wool at 106 percent of

In 1955, before becoming a Senate Page Boy, the author, then 15, met Senator Douglas during the Senator's visit to Kentucky.

Bobby Baker, left, was Assistant Secretary for the Minority Party in the Senate when the above picture was taken of the 25-year-old South Carolinian talking to Felton Johnson, Minority Party Secretary. In 1956 the Democrats became the Majority Party and Baker became Secretary for the Majority—the shining example of a Senate Page Boy who made good. At the same time Felton Johnson became the Secretary of the Senate. *Wide World Photos*

Senator Styles Bridges of New Hampshire and Everett Dirksen of Illinois make plans for the first conference of Republican senators at the beginning of the second session of the 84th Congress. *Wide World Photos*

Former President Hoover talks with Senator John F. Kennedy, then starting his first term in the Senate, before the start of a hearing concerning the work load of the President (January, 1956). *Wide World Photos*

Senators William A. Fulbright, John Sparkman, Hubert Humphrey, Mike Mansfield, Alben Barkley and Wayne Morse at a hearing on the administration's Middle East Arms Policies, a major foreign affairs problem in 1956. *Wide World Photos*

Chairman John McClellan of the Senate Investigations Subcommittee points a finger as he speaks out at trade control inquiry. Shown with him are Senator Sam Ervin, Senator Henry Jackson, subcommittee counsel Robert Kennedy, and Senator Joseph McCarthy. (March 9, 1956) *Wide World Photos*

Vice-President Richard Nixon holds a copy of a farm bill as he poses with Senator Roman Hruska and Senator Carl Curtis (March 1956) in his office. *Wide World Photos*

Senator Barry Goldwater, GOP Chairman Leonard Hall, Senator John Kennedy and Democratic Chairman Paul Butler appear on a political panel before 3,000 delegates of the United States Chamber of Commerce annual meeting, May 1, 1956. *Wide World Photos*

Senator Margaret Chase Smith and Mrs. Eleanor Roosevelt shake hands after appearing on a television program where they had disagreed sharply on U.S. foreign policy. *Wide World Photos*

Senators Hubert Humphrey and William Knowland listen to a debate in the United Nations General Assembly, December 19, 1956. *Wide World Photos*

Senate Majority Leader Lyndon B. Johnson talks with House Speaker Sam Rayburn at the Democratic State Convention (1956) in Fort Worth, Texas. *Wide World Photos*

At a party in Chicago given by Sam Rayburn, the top contenders for the Democratic Presidential Nomination, Adlai Stevenson and Averell Harriman, pose with Senate Majority Leader Lyndon B. Johnson and his mother, Mrs. Sam Johnson (August 13, 1956). *Wide World Photos*

Former President Harry S Truman stands with Adlai Stevenson and Estes Kefauver at the Democratic Convention in Chicago where they were named as their parties' presidential and vice-presidential candidates. Truman had just announced his support of Stevenson and Kefauver. *Wide World Photos*

parity because wool is produced in his home state of Utah. The charge is so unfounded and was so ineptly delivered that it was pathetic. The Senator seemed to enjoy his little joke, however, and we must not treat it lightly, for this was his entire contribution to the round of questioning and was the result of an hour of intense concentration and penetrating analysis of Benson's testimony.

Hours and hours of the past week were spent in a Democratic postmortem on the farm bill. Reactions ranged from vicious personal attacks to heart-rending sob stories. And so it was with the utmost difficulty that anything at all was accomplished legislatively. The pending business skidded recklessly from Monday until the final vote on Thursday, and hardly a word was spoken on the measure itself.

While this bill may have no great intrinsic importance, it is a very graphic illustration of how senators stand on certain issues. The bill as reported from the Foreign Relations Committee provided for an unqualified increase in our contribution to the International Labor Organization. This seemed a fairly innocuous and routine matter until Senator Bricker decided to stick his pudgy finger into the pie. He proposed an amendment to the appropriation stating that the United States would immediately lower its contributions drastically if the Communists were permitted to vote in the organization, as they do at present.

Up until now our support has had no strings attached, though there has been some dissatisfaction with various aspects of the organization. Our government has entered wholeheartedly into its spirit and work and has tried to create the impression that the United States is just one of the gang, working together with others in a spirit of friendship. The Senator's amendment proposes to squash this feeling entirely and to substitute for it the uneasy feeling that "Well, of course you understand that we don't trust you, and aren't very happy about the whole thing, but we'll sort of hedge along, maybe offering you a few tidbits from the table now and then." Many conscientious senators saw and said that it would be vastly better for us to withdraw from the organization completely than to continue as members under such conditions, which would put the United States in the position of the vengeful rich uncle who is waiting for the first opportunity to cut the relatives out of the loot.

Naturally the administration, which has charge of our foreign policy, opposed the Bricker amendment, and yet only six of the 47 Senate Republicans voted with the Republican administration. The other Republicans, joining forces with the Southern conservatives, mustered a sufficient margin to pass the amendment. It would seem that Eisenhower is the President without a party.

As Lyndon Johnson said the other day, "When someone asked me what were the main duties of the Majority Leader, I told him, to protect the President's foreign policy—particularly from Republicans."

One of the most revealing things about the Senate is where the pages come from, because as a general rule the senators who control patronage also control the Senate. And a glance at the home states of the pages confirms the generally held belief that the Southern Democrats control the Senate. There are two pages from Georgia, two from Tennessee, three from Kentucky, one from Florida, one from South Carolina, one from Arkansas, one from Missouri, one from Mississippi, one from North Carolina, one from Oklahoma, and a handful from places ranging from Maine to Oregon. There are a surprising number of Kentuckians on the official staff of the Senate. The Chief Clerk is from Whitesburg, the File Clerk is a Kentuckian and the personal secretary to the Secretary of the Senate is the sister of a former Kentucky governor.

The coming of Senator T., to fill out the term of the late Senator P., has confirmed the saying that you aren't a senator when you come here, that you have to learn to be a senator. He has been wandering around in a daze, trying to remember the names of the 95 senators who have introduced themselves to him and trying to be polite to Nixon, who gave him a condescending pat on the back and said patronizingly, "I think you will find this an interesting and valuable experience."

His way is strewn with many obstacles. He knows he is here for only six months because the Governor who appointed him is a candidate in the election this fall. He therefore cannot very well fire the office staff of the late Senator and hire his own for that short period. Unfortunately this staff presents quite a number of problems to the inexperienced legislator. To begin with, the administrative assistant wanted the appointment to fill out the term himself. Then there is the aggrieved Mrs. P., aggrieved not only at the loss of her husband but also because she was not chosen to fill out the term. She is a God-fearing woman and therefore considers herself qualified for the job. She has taken advantage of her sorrow to torment the office staff, lording it over the office and pleading the immunity of the afflicted to any appeals that she lay off. Poor Senator T. has been forced to use Bobby Baker's office to answer his mail.

April 27, 1956

The "do-nothing" 84th Congress has been doing nothing lately primarily because there has been nothing to do. There just wasn't anything on the calendar to discuss, except Bricker's proposed Constitutional amendment, which won't be called up anyway. Beside a few appropriation bills and an occasional bill of passing interest nothing has been accomplished since the Easter recess. This situation was dramatized by a letter that Lyndon Johnson sent to each committee chairman, urging him to hurry up and report something for the Senate to argue about.

Last week was spent in lethargic and dispirited recrimination over the President's veto of the farm bill. And again on Tuesday of this week there was nothing to discuss, so the unquenchable fires, like Senator Humphrey, sputtered over Lyndon Johnson's radio-television address, in which he answered for the Democrats the President's farm-veto message to the nation. What this debate lacked in vital importance it supplied in frayed dispositions. Senator Kerr has many fine fiery qualities, among which lovableness is not outstanding. Indeed lovableness is so little in evidence in Senator Kerr that he completely antagonized lovable Homer Capehart of Indiana. Senator Kerr is a brilliant, dynamic, incisive debater and loves nothing better than to tear just about everything into fine shreds, though he sometimes gets carried away in the smoke of his own excitement; Senator Capehart offers the Senate's broadest expanse as a target.

The week cannot be counted a total loss legislatively because the Senate passed the bank-holding bill, which defines and provides for the regulation of companies controlling major portions of two or more banks. At present there are 46 such concerns. There is a certain significance in the manner in which the bill reached its final form.

The bill in its original form, as introduced by Senator Bricker, Ohio's chubby conservative, was a fairly simple one providing that a bank-holding company could not engage in business activities not integrally connected with banking. That the need for such legislation was generally acknowledged is attested by the very fact that Senator Bricker introduced the bill. He would generally be the last one to support a bill providing for governmental regulation of private enterprise.

Senator Douglas pointed out the basic reasons for the need for increased regulation of bank-holding companies. He showed that the three largest banks in Canada control 67 percent of total deposits. He argued that this concentration of financial power in banking leads to monopolies in other fields of industry and that such potent uncontrolled power centers in the economy can have dire results. He stated that it was through the backing of certain key financial organizations that Hitler came to power in Germany. The need is thus seen for some type of regulation for bank-holding companies.

There are further arguments dealing with the specific type of regulation Senator Bricker is advocating. I understand that it is common practice for bank-holding companies to venture into other fields of industry. For instance, one of the largest insurance companies in the country is owned by a bank-holding company. It is quite conceivable that the depositors' funds might be channeled off into this secondary field of endeavor and risked in ventures that might lead to injury to the bank depositor and to the affected industry, since the concern controlling the bank and the company would not have to worry about interest rates.

I mentioned that I felt that the way the bill was handled was

98

significant. The Banking and Currency Committee was not content to report out the Senator's bill in the innocuous form in which it was received. The Committee felt that a couple of other provisions, which other groups wanted, should be combined with it. And so it was that the bill as reported to the floor from the Committee provided that no bank-holding company could expand without the approval of the Federal Reserve Board. Senator Bricker was beginning to feel a little uneasy about the eventual effect of his harmless little bill by this time. Not only was the bank-holding company to be deprived of its extracurricular activities, but it also would have to get approval from the dean before taking on an extra class load. The Senator was not at all sure that this did not constitute an indefensible invasion of individual and corporate liberty. He became firmly convinced, however, when the next provision was added to the bill, this time by floor amendment.

Senator Douglas is always on the lookout for opportunities to tie things onto legislation. He decided to attempt to put more teeth in the regulation. The Senator's intentions were certainly spotless enough, but his amendment, which was passed, approached the problem from the wrong standpoint. His provision stated that no bank-holding company could expand across state lines without special consent of the state involved. Since no state allows this at present, passage would be tantamount to putting a clamp on the expansion of the bank-holding companies. As Senator Bennett pointed out, this amendment is predicated on the assumption that a bank-holding company is considered evil and undesirable until it can prove itself an asset. The Senator from Utah foresaw that inequities might arise from the state's power of exclusion, which could lead to preferential treatment and discrimination.

Whatever the defects of the amendment, it certainly fulfilled its purpose of further limiting the bank-holding companies. Thus Senator Bricker was violently opposed to the final version of his innocuous piece of legislation.

Harry Gold, a convicted espionage agent who sold atomic secrets to Russia, is a remorseful little man with close-cropped convict-type black hair and a pathetic defenseless expression. Herman Welker is a senator from Idaho, with magnified ideas about his importance, his sagacity and his potential worth. These two gentlemen ran into each other at an Internal Security subcommittee meeting probing the Rosenberg affair. Welker took this opportunity to display his great perception of human nature and his noble compassion. "Was it worth it?" he asked. He wound up the hearing with a display of feigned superior dignity. With liquor giving a heavy accent to each word, he said in essence, "Now aren't you ashamed of yourself?" He spoke with disgust, which he evidently was trying to make do for hauteur. Then he waved Gold aside with airy grandeur, looking very wise and very, very foolish.

April 28, 1956

On Saturday afternoon I went to a Stevenson rally. The District primary is on Tuesday, and the Stevenson people are putting on a flurried last-ditch effort. The celebrities were manifold. Movie-star Myrna Loy read telegrams from various other celebrities regretting that they could not be present. Senators Murray of Montana and Neuberger of Oregon were present. When the hat had been passed and the brass band had been going relentlessly for a while, we came to the feature attraction, the "greatest woman in the world, for many years this country's first lady and now first lady of the world." I understand that there was a good deal of scheming back of the appearance of Mrs. Roosevelt in the District just before Adlai goes to the polls. They say that the dynamic former First Lady is almost worshiped in most Negro homes in the District as the first occupant of the White House to take their interests to heart. And when one considers that about 60 percent of the residents of the District (not to mention suburbs in Virginia and Maryland) are colored, Mrs. Roosevelt's swooping down to pat Adlai on his bald head just before the primary takes on quite a bit of significance.

Mrs. Roosevelt was well aware of her mission. Most of her

speech was on civil rights. Her two main points were that civil rights has become much more than a domestic issue—it has become the testing ground for whether or not we can maintain our leadership of the world, which is two-thirds nonwhite (at this point the Negro lady beside me started clapping impulsively)—and that Adlai Stevenson is basically a man of honor and understanding who will live up to his commitments in the field of civil rights. She also mentioned seeing him in action on his trip around the world after his defeat in 1952. She was impressed by his immediate understanding of people and their cordial response to him. She said that Eisenhower was "a good man, but . . . ," smiling winningly. Her voice broke with amusement at many points. She beat her companions to the car by several lengths.

Since nothing was rolling along merrily on the Senate floor on Monday, I was forced to seek diversion elsewhere, and, since elsewhere the Secretary of State was having his usual difficulties with certain Democratic senators, diversion was just around the corner.

Dulles came before the Foreign Relations Committee on Monday morning as lead-off man for the Administration's mutual-security program. The program that he outlined in a statement couched in singularly bad English took this form: 83 percent for frankly military strengthening of our allies in Formosa, Indochina and Europe and 17 percent for economic assistance.

The granting of a foreign-aid appropriation is a very complicated procedure. The Foreign Relations Committee authorizes a certain amount, the Appropriations Committee then appropriates a certain amount, the Congress usually approves that amount and the Executive spends a certain amount. It is possible for these amounts to be entirely different. For instance, last year the State Department spent 40 percent more than was authorized and appropriated.

The request presented by the Executive was $4.2 billion, approximately 40 percent greater than was authorized last year. It is, however, about what was actually spent by the administration, which grossly overreached its allotted appropriation. Secretary Dulles insisted that the increased authorization would only main-

101

tain our present program at its current level. So, Secretary Dulles concluded, there should be no griping about appropriating the additional sum.

Senator Fulbright delights in antagonizing and confounding people and takes great pride in his ability to do so. He asked the Secretary how he would distribute his funds if he were given 40 percent less than he asked for. Dulles was dumbfounded. "Do you think it is such a fantastic suggestion," prodded the good Senator with ill-concealed pleasure, "that we might give you what you received last year?" The Secretary was silent for a very long time. He avoided coming to grips with the issue, or perhaps it might be more accurate to say that he stumbled around the brink of the issue. He tried to avoid committing himself, and, although he did not make any quotable assertion, his inadroit attempts at expression and subterfuge made it plain that he considered military much more vital than economic assistance.

Fulbright had the elephant tied down and proceeded to tickle its trunk. His argument went something like this: I'm an elected official. I have constituents. On the one hand the President, Vice-President and Secretary of State are telling my constituents that we are in the golden age of peace and prosperity. On the other, I must go to them and say that the Congress has decided that the world situation is so critical and that our security is so vitally threatened that they must add 40 percent to the foreign-aid appropriation. Whom are they to believe? Me or the President and Secretary of State? Well, of course, I hope that they will believe me.

I was sitting about fifteen feet from the Secretary when Fulbright made that last statement. He reared back in his chair and looked as if he were about to throw the mike at the glib, smiling Senator. It was the first time I really felt that he was mad. Dulles flatly and civilly retorted that the increased appropriation would not be an increased expenditure, as the administration had been spending that larger amount already.

At other points in the hearing as well, I felt that Dulles fell rather short as a parrier. Morse asked him if more of the 17 percent of economic aid could not be administered through the United Nations. Dulles very probably was correct in his assertion that it would be

102

impractical at this time. But he made no attempt to back up that statement; he just made it. This gave the strong impression that he was exasperated, on the defensive. Also Senator Knowland asked him why it was that Soviet loans get more favorable publicity than United States gifts. Dulles said that Soviet loans were more newsworthy than United States gifts because they were more uncommon. Again he merely made that statement and did not try to suggest a remedy.

As nothing was also happening on the floor after lunch, I went to the hearings conducted by the Special Investigating Committee on the Air Force, which has been making its presence felt lately under the chairmanship of Senator Symington. General Curtis LeMay, Commander of the Strategic Air Command, was the witness. Everything was rigged in advance. The questions had been submitted to him the day before, and he had cleared his written answers with the Defense Department, so nothing spectacular could be anticipated. The General is chubby, has a shock of black hair, is dour and studious in appearance and is precise but not emphatic in speech. It gave a very strange sensation to think that what he was saying was that United States air supremacy might be lost in two years, yet he said it in the manner you generally associate with the treasurer of the local Lions Club giving the financial report. All such statements seem to be along the same lines these days: The Communists are making phenomenal strides forward, but we are still gallantly holding on to the lead in everything by the skin of our incomparable teeth.[3]

By this time it was worth the trip back to the Senate floor to hear the Vice-President of Brazil give the usual "Greetings from one great country to another" routine in Portuguese. Very educational. He was diplomatic enough to work in a plug for both Roosevelt and Eisenhower. Then came the Barkley news, which filled the evening.

When I was in Kentucky, I assured people that in all probability Senator Barkley would live out his term with ease. He died

[3] The tone of such statements was to change not long after, following the Russian launching of Sputnik in 1957.

103

less than a week after that. Fifteen minutes later, all Capitol flags were at half-mast.

I am sure that anyone would have given the same answer I gave. Last week at the Wilson Day banquet he held spellbound for thirty minutes an audience that had chatted discourteously through other addresses. Also last week he introduced a resolution to improve drastically certain Senate procedures, and, when it was read, the senators actually applauded because it was such an obvious, simple and worthwhile change.

That evening we stayed in the Clements office answering phone calls from snoopers ("When did you hear him speak last?"), sympathizers, sensationalists ("I expected as much") and senators until 7:30, when we decided it was useless and went home. What made the entire situation so confused was that Senator Clements had left for Washington from Kentucky, where he had made a speech at Mt. Sterling, and was due in Washington early the next morning, but we in the office did not know how and when he was traveling. We had to put off the Associated Press by saying that we hadn't the slightest idea how the Senator could be reached.

The Barkley funeral on Wednesday at the Foundry Methodist Church, with Senate Chaplain Frederick Brown Harris in charge of the service, was attended *en masse* by the Kentucky congressional delegation (page division), numbering three. It was the most celebrity-infested occasion I have witnessed. The service was very fine indeed. Dr. Harris is a stirringly earnest and appealingly unpretentious speaker.

I saw at least sixty senators in attendance. There may have been more. Sam Rayburn and Dean Acheson were there. We three pages sat squarely in the middle of the specially reserved congressional section. Sitting beside me in our row were Scott Lucas, who had followed Barkley as Majority Leader from 1949 to 1950, and Congressman James Roosevelt. Sitting in the row in front of us were the eight Kentucky congressmen in a group. In the next row forward sat Vice-President Nixon with a cordon of Secret Service men. In the third row forward from us and about six feet away from me sat Dwight D. Eisenhower, Sherman Adams and James

Hagerty. There may be some significance in the fact that Nixon sat in the row behind the Presidential party and Ike never even looked in his direction. Hagerty did have a word or two with him.

To me, the remarkable thing about the funeral was not that such a vast number of conspicuous men were present, but that they were inconspicuous. The President came in with a small group, and if he had not been staring me right in the face I might have missed him entirely. Senators, the Vice-President, *et al.*, filed in quietly and unceremoniously. The other day I went back to the National Presbyterian Church to see if Reverend Elson prayed for five minutes for the President even when he wasn't there. He did. There was no such uneasy feeling of awareness at Barkley's funeral. Perhaps it was because Dr. Harris has a profound disregard for party labels and official titles. The sanctuary was so silent that the occasional subdued click of a camera from the back of the room was very loud.

The Senate was in session for four hours and ten minutes this week: four hours on Monday and ten minutes on Thursday to pass a sympathy resolution. This compares with a maximum this year of forty hours in session, which is formidable when you remember that we convene at twelve noon; it means an average of 8:00 P.M. adjournment since we work only five days a week.

May 10, 1956

I learned today all about the workings of the Democratic Policy Committee, through which the party organization runs the Senate. At a majority conference the Democrats pick three senators to represent the party. These three are chiefly responsible for picking other members of the committees and, being on all committees, are in a position to guide and coordinate party activities. Senator Hennings, one of the three, is Secretary of the Conference, whose duty is to see that the various committees are not stepping on one another's toes. The two others are Lyndon Johnson and Earle Clements.

These three senators are the only ones who serve on both Democratic committees, the Steering Committee and the Policy Committee. The Steering Committee is the body that makes assignments to the standing committees of the Senate. The duties of the Policy Committee are more varied. Some years ago a party would hold a caucus, debate a certain issue and take a vote within the party; then the majority decision was considered binding on all members present, and all were expected to vote with the majority. As the Democratic and Republican parties became unrecognizable masses of compromise, however, this system became impracticable. The Policy Committee is the successor to the party caucus. It consists of nine members. Membership is jealously coveted, and its roster reads like a seniority list. Senators who are second, third, fifth, and sixth in seniority are members. Only two senators with six years of service are on the committee, Hennings of Missouri and Clements.

The basic function of the Committee is to decide when (and whether) to schedule major legislation. In connection with this function, it discusses important issues affecting the Senate and Democrats in general and arrives at stands on various questions, but it cannot issue an "official" Democratic position, as was done after party caucuses. In place of the tyrannical, binding control of the majority rule in the party caucus there is a device labeled "Earle Clements." As Assistant Majority Leader, he has to try to bring about some measure of unity within the party on major issues. This means that he is continually contacting individual senators concerning various matters.

The Committee's staff prepares digests of every bill before the Senate, maintains the voting records of all senators and wrote Lyndon Johnson's reply to Eisenhower's farm-bill veto.

Through Wednesday of this week, floor action centered around the Capital Transit Company, the outfit that runs the streetcars. Debate was arrestingly dull. Beside all this great unexcitement, the following should be noted: I was requisitioned by the Republicans to move and cull the individual voting records that they keep for campaign fodder. A large stack labeled "Hon. Alben W. Barkley" was discarded as no longer useful.

106

On Tuesday this year's coyest candidate, New York's favorite millionaire, Averell Harriman, was in town and was caught in the act of being coy. Well backed by the back-room boys from Tammany, he was testifying about various flood projects before the Appropriations Committee. He made a very fine impression and was most charming. He sympathized with Carl Hayden ("the Father of Reclamation") about the difficulties of persuading farmers to allow their land to be flooded. When he left the committee room, the reporters were waiting, with massive spotlights and me staring him right in the eye. He displayed a refreshing, boyish delight and uncertainty about where to stand and what to do to accommodate the cameramen. He smiled and remonstrated with the newsmen for trying to get something new out of him when his status of active passivity had not changed. Yet the candidate, looking not much older and much more intelligent than this year's most cloying candidate, Estes Kefauver, was obviously pleased with his new toy.

Tuesday evening I dropped my studious demeanor and Carlyle's *French Revolution* and picked up the banner that had been lying idle since the Stevenson rally. This time the banner read "Well Done Lyndon." The occasion was the return to Washington of the "victory twins," better known as Rayburn and Johnson, after their smashing victory in the fight for control of the Texas delegation. Most of the Democratic pages were on hand to hoist gigantic billboards bearing such messages as I have indicated. A surprisingly large crowd was on hand, well stocked with Capitol employees. A small brass aggregation gave spirit to the occasion. Nine-year-old Lucy Johnson, whom I have mentioned before, was writhing with pleasure. She had in tow the family dog.

The Senator was genuinely moved by the enthusiastic reception, and all during Rayburn's address he pondered the sign that read "Johnson for President" and the one with the ten-gallon hat reading "Throw It In, Lyndon." And, when he got around to saying the inevitable few words, he spoke like a candidate. "We went to the people and told them the truth, and they embraced it. . . . I do not consider it a personal victory, but a victory for moderation."

As the two Texans stepped from the plane and as they traversed

107

the forty-foot red carpet to the microphones, of which I had a commanding view from my perch in the bass horn, it was impossible to see or hear anything in the mob of several hundred people, all trying desperately to unseat me. So we yelled and waved and got in people's way to make up for it. The Senator almost got bopped on the head with one of our signs, but I doubt that he would have noticed.

If for no other reason, Johnson will never be President because he is by far the most unphotogenic person I have ever seen. As in the photograph that was published of the reception, he always looks sickly and as though he is about to faint from exhaustion. In person, he is tall and handsome with a deep Texas tan, a stupendous wardrobe and a gentle, reserved disposition. Conversely, it is conceivable that Nixon may some day be President because he is most photogenic. In person, beside his personality traits, he has a long nose, and when he presides he does so in an ungodly slump. In his pictures he is much better looking. To get back to the picture of Johnson's reception, in back is a House page. The sign is much inferior to the ones we were carrying, only the corners of which are visible. I am about three feet out of the picture.

May 17, 1956

Floor action was decidedly on the upswing this week, with two major pieces of legislation keeping the Senate at work until seven every day. Three days were spent on the Lehman bill. Long before it was taken up Lehman was hovering around the chamber. He had his lunch brought up by a page and ate in the cloakroom to ensure that nothing would go wrong. This bill of his will be of major importance to him in his campaign for re-election this year, if he runs. It would authorize the State of New York to develop the water resources of Niagara Falls as provided for in the United States–Canadian treaty of 1950. Senator Lehman made a good case, and after the first day his presentation had made it clear that development by the New York Power Authority was the only alternative. He stressed that Dewey, Eisenhower, Roosevelt and

Harriman favor this plan. He said that the plan was the overwhelming choice of the people of New York. He showed that electric rates in Canada, utilizing the falls through a public agency, are one-half of United States rates. And from TVA he demonstrated that the profits of private companies actually go up with the development of public projects. So my mind was unruffled at the end of the first day. It seemed not so much a question of public versus private power as it was a question of whether to bow to the wishes of the State of New York. It seemed perfectly logical to let the state develop Niagara in the way it saw fit. But, as Senator Allott, a Republican, said to me when we discussed the matter, "There are a lot of things Lehman didn't mention."

Some of those things came out in the first opposition speech made by the senior Senator from New York, Irving Ives, Republican. He also supported public development of the Niagara, but he was opposed to certain restrictions that Lehman had written into the bill to provide for public development. One such restriction was the provision that preference in service was to be given to city and state organs. This provision Ives considered rank discrimination against private enterprise and an attempt to dictate to New York State.

An interesting example of senatorial confusion resulted from the Niagara debate. As I said, Ives agreed with Lehman on the question of public development; he only objected to certain provisions in the authorization of that public development. Yet, as part of his complete rebuttal of Senator Lehman, he felt it necessary to question him on the general issue of public versus private power. His argument went something like this: "While I also support public development, it would be perfectly possible for me to support private development. Some of the arguments for private development are such and such." This sort of thing is dangerous because it generally takes half an hour for a persistent senator to get another back on the track, fifteen minutes of which are spent in assuring the offended senator that all in all he is making a superlative statement.

This line of attack on the part of Ives suggested that he was himself not sure of his disagreement with the bill. Senator Kerr criticized him for not submitting an amendment, asking him if he had writer's cramp.

Herbert Lehman, who looks like a bald bulldog, is another one of the endless variety of character studies the Senate affords. He can only be described as an intensely dedicated man, devoted to civil rights and liberalism in general and to efforts to bring about civil-rights and welfare legislation. It is my impression that his serious-minded persistence has made him feel that his achievements are insufficient. It would appear that he has what borders on an inferiority complex, something incredible in a person who was Governor of New York for ten years. Perhaps the term "insufficiency" is better than "inferiority." His eagerness and complete lack of sense of humor (which might distract him from the Cause) give him the appearance of a little boy hopefully and apprehensively offering a present to the head of a gang he hopes to join. His amateurish speaking efforts add to this impression. Senator Lehman speaks like a man delivering an awkward uppercut to the jaw and then standing back open-mouthed to see what happens.

After the Senator gave his speech to an enthralled audience of two, his administrative assistant felt called upon to console the Senator, worried over his failure to attract a larger audience. The bill was passed, but only after Senators Kefauver and Morse flew in from Oregon, Clements from Kentucky and Kennedy from Massachusetts just for the vote. Lyndon Johnson did some fancy rounding up at the last minute. It would appear that he is also interested in retaining a Democratic seat in New York this election year.

When Senator Bob Kerr of Oklahoma delivers a speech, all Capitol employees drop whatever they are doing or talking about and race for the Senate floor. Policy makers in the Policy Committee, Lyndon's secretaries, doormen and administrative assistants come panting in, licking their chops in anticipation of the kill. You can never tell what Battling Bob will say (he never uses a prepared text), but you can be sure that there will be several corpses by the time he is through. Kerr will leave even the most obdurate opponent grasping for his reeling desk. It is an unspoken rule that we never put Kerr's glass of water on the desk where he is speaking—always on the one beside it. When Kerr's arms start flailing and pounding, it takes him some time to unwind, and by that time the debris is widespread.

Today's poor dumbfounded target was Republican Capehart of Indiana, whose greatest victory lately has been at poker. Kerr said that today's debate excelled even the great capacity of the Senator from Indiana to confuse the issue. He said that when the Senator from Indiana says he is a farmer it is easy to believe because of the amount of hogwash he has indulged in today. There were myriad other things that lose luster in retelling or are not what one might call proper or are only effective when delivered by the Senator in person.

Votes in the Senate are always rigged and often farcical. There are two examples from this week. First, the presiding officer said, "All in favor say 'aye' "; silence; "All opposed, 'no' "; silence; "The 'ayes' have it."

Then the most uproarious one happened Wednesday night at 7:00 P.M., just as the Senate was preparing to adjourn. Johnson asked for speedy passage of a routine money bill. At the time, following the main vote of the evening, there were only twenty Republicans and ten Democrats left on the floor. Democrat Humphrey was presiding. When the "ayes" were called for, the ten Democrats made a respectable noise. When the "nos" were requested, the twenty Republicans obviously made more noise. But, as Humphrey knew that the bill was scheduled to pass, he said, "The 'ayes' have it." The Republicans requested a division, in which all senators stand to be counted on a vote. Now as everyone realizes it is rather a touchy matter to say that ten Democrats outnumber twenty Republicans, Johnson went to work fast. And, while the Parliamentarian spent thirty seconds counting each senator, as instructed, Johnson had a little word with Senator Knowland, Minority Leader. He told him that he knew perfectly well that the Democrats could pass this bill if they got all their senators there, but it was simply being ornery to force all of them to come back for a vote. Knowland had no real desire to be unpleasant and unreasonable, so the request for division was withdrawn,

111

and again they had a voice vote. Again the "nos" completely drowned out the "ayes." "The 'ayes' have it," said Senator Humphrey.

Senator Kefauver, back from a month of groveling among the rabble, is the most tanned senator. Senator Pastore, back from a month's inspection of the Pacific, is a close second.

At 12:20 on Thursday the Senate adjourned, and senators and pages marched, two abreast, through the Capitol. A madding crowd was jamming the rotunda to see us go by. We waved and smiled at the assembled multitude. "Oh, look," cried one impressionable lady, "here come the pages. Aren't they cute?" We demurred. We entered the House chamber, where Nixon and Rayburn had two chairs side by side on the rostrum. Pages and senators took their respective places. Yelled a black-garbed gentleman in the aisle, "Mr. Speaker, the Ambassadors." In trooped fifty of the aforementioned. "Mr. Speaker, the Supreme Court." In filed Warren & Co., outfitted in flowing robes. "Mr. Speaker, the President's Cabinet." In bounced Wilson and Summerfield and some others I did not recognize. "Mr. Speaker, the President of Indonesia." A handsome man, dressed in a plain white military-type suit and a black cap entered, followed by the escorting committee, Senators Knowland, Johnson, Wiley and George. The Senate, the House, the Cabinet, the Supreme Court and the pages rose to give the President a standing ovation.

Sukarno was introduced by Mr. Speaker Rayburn. The regally attired attendant at the side of his unribboned master handed him his speech. Then he handed him his glasses, then his glass of water. Thus equipped, he was ready to begin. The speech was delivered in English. He stumbled only once, repeating "indivisible" several times, always incorrectly, before giving up. At one point in his speech he started to outline the five principles on which he said his nation was based. One, belief in God; at this point we all applauded appropriately. Two, humanity; we all applauded vigorously and were only waiting for him to voice the third to let out another round of applause. Three, nationalism; the applause started up as usual, then died with a sickly gasp. Sukarno blithely

112

went on to four, democracy, and thankfully the audience was able to give this a hearty hand. And to five, justice. He stated that his country was seriously engrossed in self-realization and was ready to accept aid from any quarter with the condition that such aid would not involve any loss of recently won and jealously cherished sovereignty.

May 24, 1956

That Senator Barkley's place as Chairman of the Democratic Senatorial Campaign Committee has not been filled yet is important. That for the first time on record Senators Morse and Stennis (of Oregon and Mississippi) agreed, in their praise of Senator Barkley, is significant. Senator Barkley was that rarity in the Democratic Party, a moderate man. The best example of his moderation that I have witnessed was when Senator Eastland of Mississippi was due to become Chairman of the Judiciary Committee. On that occasion, Morse and Stennis went riding off on their high horses, and it took a commanding "whoa" from Senator Barkley to bring some reason to the discussion. Senator Barkley had little sympathy for the Southern conservative position. Yet he took the command of the Campaign Committee, which is supposed to succor North and South alike. Whether he learned it or whether he came by it naturally, Senator Barkley grasped the importance of laughter; he had learned that it is remarkable what can be said about an opponent with a smile. It seemed perfectly natural and not at all disrespectful that a group of Senate employees the other day were trying to recall what was the last dirty joke that Senator Barkley told them. The one they finally decided upon centered around two unsavory bums named "Ike" and "Milt."

Senator George's decision not to run again brought a universal sigh of relief. It was the only judicious alternative. All the Georgians on the Hill whom I have talked to agreed that the Senator would have been defeated by Herman Talmadge in this years' primary. Senator Barkley's death precipitated the announcement in two ways. First, politically, the death of the "Iron Man" was going

113

to create grave and vocal doubts in the mind of Herman about the staying power of the aging George. Second, personally, Barkley dined almost daily with George in the office of the Secretary of the Senate. In Senator Barkley, George lost his only contemporary. Although most senators are on first-name terms with one another, the senior senator from Georgia is always "Senator George," never "Walter."

I have been trying to discover for some time just what the contribution of senators like George and Murray of Montana is. Obviously the actual work they perform is negligible. Frequently Senator George spends his afternoons dozing on the Senate floor. What I have been trying to discover is just how genuine is their reputed vast store of knowledge and experience. This problem is increased by the fact that both these senators have marvelous staffs, people with responsible judgment and with years of experience in the senators' fields. It is often impossible to detect to what extent a statement comes from the senator personally. I have heard Senator George speak on the Senate floor extemporaneously, albeit infrequently. I have seen him preside at meetings of the Foreign Relations Committee. What he says is invariably sensible, but it takes him forever to get it out.

While I have reached no final decisions in the matter, I can mention some of the distinct advantages of having a few "sacred cows" around. It may be all right to debunk prestige, to disparage the infallible wisdom of an exhausted old man like Senator George, yet those tarnished attributes still remain to be reckoned with. Prestige is very important; a name is the product only of years of effort. While the statements of Senator George may be written by Senators Fulbright or Thurmond, while they may be commonplace, nevertheless, as statements by Senator George, they carry weight. When Senator George went to the White House to discuss with the President his plan for long-term foreign aid, the Senator made no statement upon his departure. Headlines the next day read, "George stands firm on aid." In other words, George didn't say anything. The Senate Chaplain said the next day, "Senator, you're the only man I know of who can make headlines by not saying anything." And he was right.

114

Washington is, of course, beautiful these days. There is some sort of Oriental shrub that is a mass of shocking pink. Everything is flawless green, shocking pink, cloudless blue and so on. There are also dandelions in the grass in the Supreme Court lawn, which is reassuring.

Not having seen a really bad play in ages, I was naturally intrigued by the reviews of *Thieves' Paradise*, currently showing at the Shubert. It was variously described in such telling phrases as "Nightmarish fable . . . paralyzing dullness . . . as stupefying an exhibit as has donned the mask of drama in seasons. . . . As author of *Thieves' Paradise*, Mr. Fagan is not only a hard man to follow, but also lacks the knack of suggesting he would be worth it . . . perilously deficient. . . . It would imperil one's sanity to venture in the labyrinth of the play's intrigue. . . . It can be said, however, that the actors behave with the hesitation of high school students who have taken over world government for a day. . . . This has a way of intensifying the confusion of *Thieves' Paradise* which does not need another wisp of haze to make it the murkiest offering of its year." We were naturally eager to go, and, when the play was so poorly attended that $3 tickets were being given away, a group of us went and had a rousing time. It turned out, as reported, to be a professional production of colossal idiocy.

The play's basic proposition was that Molotov and Generalissimo Roosevelt had formed the United Nations at Yalta in order that the United States might eventually become merely a unit in the United Nations framework and therefore completely at the mercy of the Russian overlords of the United Nations; that General Eisenhower sold East Germany and the Balkans to the Russians; that General Marshall sold out to the Russians in China, and that General MacArthur in Korea relayed his plans to Washington, where they were given to North Korea. "That means," exclaims one actress in horror, "that all those boys killed in Korea were actually murdered by the U.N."

This revealing bit of historical nonsense formed the basis of the play's action. If everything attributed to the Russians by this play (the buying of America's leaders, the control of the United Na-

115

tions, the winning of some unnamed "multimillionaire traitors") were actually true, I would without hesitation jump into the Communist camp, for they would be the unquestioned masterminds of the age.

These "facts" are all related to a member of the American OSS in the first scene; he is instantly convinced of their truth by various documents in the possession of the Bulgarian underground. The rest of the play revolves around the attempts of the underground to get this documentation out of Bulgaria and to the American people, so that they may wake up to the realization of what their leaders are doing to them.

After the first scene, in which Bulgarian patriots throw around names like Churchill and Roosevelt and Alger Hiss with breathtaking familiarity and breezily discuss the merits of genocide, comes unequaled confusion. Several people are meat-cleavered and a couple butcher-knifed. Add one ice pick drawn from the bosom of the heroine for indeterminate reasons; a motor boat; a dance team, and a general seasoning of MVD agents, and you get something that resembles the hopeless mess at the Shubert.

It has been suggested that the play is a plea for the Bricker amendment, but no one can really be sure what is going on.

May 25, 1956

I was about to wind up this week's account with the note that the week had been a busy but unrewarding one. I was going to comment in a desultory fashion that it was a standard week fraught with congressional stupidity and all sorts of socialism creeping through the senatorial confusion. I was going to remark that this week saw the passage of the Civil Service Retirement Act and the Housing Act, two very creepy bits of socialist legislation, and close with the prim note that pending at the end of the week was the Daniel bill to provide for more stringent control of the narcotics traffic.

The difficulty with prediction is that one cannot account for all the variables. The variable this week was Wayne Morse and his rosebud. It was thought that everyone would accept in an uncon-

116

cerned manner the invasion of rights proposed under the Daniel bill. Everyone, it was thought, realized that it was more practical to use wiretapping to catch thieves and more effective to allow the use of the death penalty. But, whatever his shortcomings, Wayne Morse is long on both principle and wind, a fatal combination. He said that he was going to postpone the vote until next week, and to dramatize his intention he pinned a rosebud on his lapel with a flourish. This called to mind the time he broke the filibuster record with a speech lasting 22 hours and 38 minutes; he said then that he would talk until the rose on his lapel wilted. This time the rosebud was only for psychological effect, however. It was necessary for him to talk only until about 6:30 on Friday to forestall any chance for a vote this week. He talked for only about three hours, of course without a text. He stressed, as though the point needed emphasis, that this was his "opening" speech on the subject.

I think I have never been so fascinated by a Senate speech. Not only because this time the speech was directed at a definite goal—postponement—but also because it was a tremendous speech. He traced down through history the precedents establishing the inviolability of the home, which he felt would be destroyed by the use of wiretapping. He gave examples from the Code of Hammurabi, from Roman law, from Cicero and from English history.

Price Daniel is an unexciting little man from Texas, who probably never heard of Hammurabi and who incidentally cannot spell. I have a note he wrote of things for me to do with some misspelled words. He is an eminently practical man and is very anxious to get his practical bill through. He argued, "But don't you realize it would be easier to use the wiretap? that all the big gangsters use the phone? that at present we are only catching the passers, not the big dealers? My plan is so practical."

Other senators don't know what to do with Wayne Morse. They keep trying to explain to him that this principle business just doesn't go over in government, but he persists in talking about morals and such nonsense. And so at the end of the week things are definitely on the upgrade; Wayne Morse and his rosebud are smiling, and Price Daniel is worriedly champing on his cigar.

117

As it turned out, Morse didn't have to filibuster after all.

Price Daniel was at one time Attorney General of Texas and has had practical experience with the narcotics traffic. Wayne Morse is a teacher, a scholar. Senator Daniel, after months of hearings, had drawn up a bill that would have made it much easier to track criminals; it provided for capital punishment and wiretapping. Wayne, however, looks askance at expedience and announced that the bill would be passed over his dead, hoarse body. When the Senate resumed consideration of the bill this Thursday, it was passed without a murmur from either side in about half an hour. This gives an excellent example of just what Bobby Baker does. He discovered by buttonholing senators that the wiretapping section of the bill would be defeated if it came to a vote on the floor. As it is his duty to save Democratic face, he whisked up to see Price Daniel, who is running for Governor of Texas this year, and laid the dismaying prospect before him. The obnoxious section was surreptitiously removed in the still of the night, and the bill sailed serenely through the Senate, *sans* wiretapping, *sans* filibuster.

We were in session thirty hours this week, 25 on Monday and Tuesday, 5 on Thursday; the 25 hours break down to eleven on Monday and fourteen on Tuesday. The road bill had to be disposed of at any cost because the Senate could not risk getting behind schedule with the narcotics bill, postponed until Thursday and promising a major fight.

Senator Laird of West Virginia, who at the end of his second month in the Senate is beginning to like the place, ruefully philosophized about the absurdity of staying up all night on Tuesday just to avoid having to do some work on Wednesday.

From now on out it will be more difficult for me to leave the floor and attend committee meetings and the like. When some senator is giving a prolonged address, it is necessary for only a couple of us to be on the floor at one time. But more and more now there will be more voting and less talking. Monday and Tuesday saw continuous voting. During a vote all the pages are needed to round up senators from hither and yon.

My only sally into foreign territory this week was a trip through the nether regions of the Joint Committee on Atomic Energy. A very elaborate set of regulations must be gone through. A friend of mine who works for the "Joint" is an authorized person, who can show people through. I had to sign the register, and my guide kept a record of the exact times of entrance and exit. A guard is at the door of the classified section night and day. He has to press various buttons to open the door-lock burglar alarm. I viewed the soundproofed executive-session room from which, at an earlier date, the first telegraph message was sent. I viewed the outside of the vaults with the classified documents. The chief counsel invited me down to talk with him about security precautions and the work of the committee. Naturally, I am putting out a feeler to the Soviet Embassy.

The longest session of the year was Tuesday (until 12:30). It was also primary time in Florida and Kentucky. One of the pages was on the phone continuously all evening, keeping senators posted on both races. Everyone was pleased when the Chandler forces were smashed. Senator Symington was very much amused and very intensely interested in the Florida vote, which kept changing and was very close all evening. Symington was in a good mood at the prospect of Adlai and Estes knocking heads and falling unconscious. At eleven or so he sent me, in a jocular way, to ask Bobby Baker if he was planning to make him stay all night. The Secretary for the Majority sent back affirmation.

A side effect of the session was that it allowed Senator Y. to get just that much more drunk. He gave up trying to make it to the door after one vote and fell over on a nearby couch.

The road-bill debate was not remarkable for its crystal clarity. Early in the day the Knowland amendment was passed. It provided that the several states would determine the wages to be paid workers on the Federally aided highways. A little later the Chavez amendment was passed. It provided that the Federal government would determine the wages to be paid workers on the Federally aided highways. When the bill came up for the vote on final passage, Senator Douglas asked what amendments he would be voting for in voting for the bill. He was assured that he would

119

be voting for everything. Senator Douglas did not appear reassured. Since the bill goes to conference I guess nothing fatal was done.

Senator Kennedy of Massachusetts could now almost pass for a college sophomore. He did not look so mature when he first came to the Senate. When he first arrived, he reportedly went in to see the Secretary of the Senate to see about his office space. The receptionist said: "Sit down, sonny. The Secretary will be able to see you in about an hour." John F. obediently sat down. One of the cloakroom assistants came by, passing through on his way to see the Secretary, and, seeing the young man wearing the dark suit and thinking him a newly arrived page, gave him some letters to mail. The Senator obliged. After a while the receptionist said: "Secretary Biffle is very busy starting the session. What do you want to see him about?" John F. said meekly, "Well, I'm Senator Kennedy, and I'd like to see about my office."

While the rest of the Senate was basking in Florida sunshine or campaigning in Kentucky, Joe McCarthy and I were slaving away in committee. For once I was in complete agreement with the junior Senator from Wisconsin, yet at the same time he slashed a dismaying gash in the gauze of my hope for his eventual rehabilitation into the brotherhood of responsible partisans. The background for this incident goes like this:

In 1940 the Smith Act was passed, relating to the prosecution of Communists. Quoting Joe: "Title 18 of the U.S. Code contains the Smith Act. Section 3231 of that Title provides that 'Nothing in this Title shall be held to take away or impair the jurisdiction of the Courts of the several states under the laws thereof.'" In 1956, in the Steve Nelson case, the Supreme Court invalidated state subversion laws, saying that by the Smith Act Congress intended to pre-empt the field of subversion legislation. In 1940 in debate on the bill and later in interpreting the law, the author of the bill, Congressman Smith of Virginia, stated repeatedly that it was not his intention to invalidate state laws. In 1956, the Supreme Court said that this was definitely Congress's intention.

The Justice Department, which administers the Act, says, "The administration of the various state laws has not, in the course of the fifteen years that the federal and state sedition laws have existed side by side, in fact interfered with, embarrassed, or impeded the enforcement of the Smith Act." The Supreme Court says the enforcement of state sedition laws "presents a serious danger of conflict with the administration of the federal program."

In 1938, Congress passed an Act on natural gas, reading, "This Act does not apply to the producers and gatherers of natural gas." In 1954, the Supreme Court said the Act did apply to the producers and gatherers of natural gas.

It just so happens that I agree in substance with what the Supreme Court decisions accomplished, but the fact remains that in so deciding the Supreme Court is clearly saying, "You don't know what you're talking about."

From this point, after outlining some of the points I have mentioned, Joe proceeded to discuss his bill, which would provide that the state had the right to prosecute reds in terms even the Supreme Court could not misconstrue. It can be argued whether this is good or not, but it would be difficult to argue that the Supreme Court has not usurped the legislative function. It can be argued that this is necessary because Congress massacres legislation, but it cannot be argued that this usurpation is not a fact.

So much for the reasons why I agree with Joe. Now for the reasons why this speech was at the same time a disillusioning blow to my blithe hopes for his rehabilitation. Joe is not the sort of person who merely states that he is in disagreement with someone. It seems that at the same time he has to impugn the virtue of his opponent. In the present instance, he went beyond the relish of the chase and spoke with what might be whispered was bad taste.

"I deeply resent . . ." the decision, said he, his monotone rising to an ominous crescendo. It is "the most flagrant instance of judicial legislation that has ever come to my attention," he added in his slightly drunken lisp. It is "outrageous. . . . The Supreme Court . . . is determined to misconstrue the law. . . . The Supreme Court was simply talking off the top of its head. . . . The majority of the judges on the present bench have apparently concluded that they are a law unto themselves."

121

He agreed with Senator Eastland's suggestion that the justices are politicians. He lamented the confirmation of the Chief Justice, unnamed, by the Congress. His argument served a useful purpose; his bill may. But his unpleasantness, hints at incrimination and personal slander were simply distasteful.

While St. John's Church is searching for a new pastor, various people are taking services. This week I went down to hear Secretary Thomas of the Navy. His talk centered on the motto of Armed Forces Day next Saturday, "Power for Peace." He stressed that the Navy has always been maintained to fight for peace. He pointed out the strong Christian tradition in the Navy. He read from the original articles governing the Navy drawn up by John Adams, which provided for services twice a day on board ship and instructed the commanding officer to take proper disciplinary action to abolish swearing. Secretary Thomas is a very poor speaker. He is short but has a long Cadillac.

In the committee at which Senator McCarthy testified, the Senator suddenly interrupted his testimony when the television spotlight was turned off. He asked the cameraman to turn the spotlight back on because he could not "read" without it.

Today I climbed to the top of the Capitol dome, where I inspected carefully the ceiling painting of George Washington, with the Graces tootling merrily on all sides. The view of the city from there is magnificent. I am a friend of the gentleman with the awesome title "Captain of the Dome."

June 7, 1956

Whether or not my appointment to the Senate was an astute move politically is open to question. I am, however, doing nothing to discourage this belief of Senator Clements, who evidently has great regard for my vote-getting potential. He returned this week from the political wars, with his primary opponent's scalp tucked prominently under his belt. Flushed with victory, he has been all smiles this week, and he congratulated me for the tremendous margin of victory in Madison County. He asked me if I had heard how large the margin was. Blushing modestly, I said, "I understand it was considerable." Then he waxed eloquent on the subject, ending up with a senatorial pat on the back for my accomplishments.

When Clements first got back on Monday, Lyndon Johnson called up and asked him to come over. Earle said he was too busy, so Johnson came over to see him.

Senator Knowland, Minority Leader, says the Senate will be out by July 17th. I am skeptical. Yet events this week on the floor made it appear that such might actually be the case. We whizzed briskly through four days of appropriation bills, never stayed past 5:00 and were not in on Friday. In fact, on Thursday they couldn't find a speaker. Or it might be more accurate to say that the only speakers they could find were the old reliables, Hubert Horatio Humphrey and Wayne Morse. Yet when Hubert had finished his daily hour-long oration (a new topic every day) and when Wayne had finished his hour-long speech in only a little more than two hours, there was nothing more to be done. If things move as smoothly as this through adjournment and if Wayne Morse can restrain himself to only two hours a day, the July 17th adjournment may not be as ridiculous as it sounds. Today Humphrey was talking about wildlife and Morse about education. Yesterday it was science and boxcars, respectively.

Senator Alexander Wiley, Republican of Wisconsin, is an amiable white-haired Eisenhower supporter, who at 72 lost the endorsement of the Republican state convention for renomination. Senator Wiley dislikes conflict and always tries to laugh off anything unpleasant. And so, while he was laughing and nervously biting his fingernails, the Republican convention proceeded to repudiate him. Ever since he has looked ghastly and has been campaigning with desperation.

On the floor Monday he made some preposterous, panic-necessitated charges against his convention-endorsed opponent. He accused his opponent of taking bribes and of accepting money from oil interests, while admitting that he didn't have any real grounds for such an accusation: "An aroma has now been arising, a not very pleasant aroma, over financial phases of the intrigue against me . . ." and so forth. This was the substance of his attack. Wiley was so nervous that he could hardly hold steady the paper he was attempting to write on.

When Senator McCarthy entered the fray, Wiley again tried to laugh it off and obscure the issue with such statements as, "Don't be too cocksure, brother." When McCarthy asked him some pertinent unpleasant questions in his usual repulsive manner, instead of answering them, Wiley said: "Now don't talk to me that way. You're not running a committee." McCarthy said: "The charge of my colleague . . . is completely false. He knows that . . . [L]et us not throw around wild and completely irresponsible charges."

Wiley said McCarthy was "meddling in my business . . . [and] as biased in this case as he is in many other cases . . . I am glad at long last that, out of the hole, certain other facts are coming. Now I know, which I did not know until right now, that the junior Senator was particeps criminis in this kind of thing."

The Big Four—Lyndon Johnson, Earle Clements, William Knowland, Styles Bridges—sat grim-faced through all this. When Wiley left, emitting small laughs of fright, no one said a word to him. Knowland went over to McCarthy, smiling with feigned relief. McCarthy wiped his brow, also sighing with relief, They exchanged a few cordial words, which definitely showed where Knowland stood in the affair.

During the past couple of days Wiley has been ostracized by the Republicans and has been trying to find solace among the Democrats. After Wiley poured out his story on the shoulder of Senator U., a Democrat, U. said to Wiley: "I agree with you that McCarthy's a louse. But you Republicans ought to stick together."

At a desk located only a few feet from those of Senator Kerr, the most forceful speaker in the Senate, and Senator Morse, one of the most brilliant senators, sits a senator who couldn't talk his way into a paper bag or think his way out. It would not be overstating it to say that Senator L. doesn't do anything. If everyone spoke as often as he does, sessions of the Senate would last about one week out of the year. Approximately every other month he reads a one-page statement. Of course, if everyone were like Senator L. nothing would ever be accomplished either. The good senator looks as if he would like nothing better than to be holding a fishing pole and chewing on a straw. He sits quietly in his corner, votes the way he's told and never says a word to anyone. He evidently hasn't the faintest notion of what is going on in his office. When I came and told him the other day that a member of his office staff was on the phone, he looked up at me blankly and, smiling mildly, said, "Are they in trouble?"

June 11, 1956

Monday night was Page Commencement. The address was by the youngest member of Congress, John Dingell, a former page. The address was very poor. He spent the first fifteen minutes telling what he was not going to say and the next five apologizing for what he had left out, and that was it. Having Commencement in a House committee room doesn't sound like much, but this committee room is really something to see, the most lavish on Capitol Hill. The 23 graduates came from seventeen states and the District. Also it isn't every Commencement that can boast the Navy orchestra and a clutch of congressmen in attendance.

Major action recently has concerned the second farm bill. Many things have been retained from the previous one but left optional on the part of the Secretary. In this way, the Democrats ostensibly bow to the wishes of the President, yet can retain a slight political advantage by saying that they gave Benson the authority to help the farmer and he did not do it. This provision made Humphrey call it a "half-baked bill."

Farm debate is always exciting. We average about one major vote each hour, which means a torrid pace for the Senate employees to round up everyone eight times daily. At eight the Senate passed one amendment 43–39, and then everyone started moaning that this would mean that the bill would be delayed in conference for a couple more weeks, and the first major squabble of the day resulted. Every attempt had been made to keep the bill free of amendments (there were forty to the last farm bill). The merits of the amendment were forgotten in an effort to get the thing over with and reconsider the amendment. For the first time Kerr agreed with Aiken, whom he had earlier called the "Black Knight from Vermont." What Aiken had said about Kerr was just as bitter but less colorful. Senator N. remarked when the two shook hands that this was as momentous as a merger of Chrysler and G.M. It took about an hour for the august Senate to come to a halt and start going backward to reconsider the vote. We also had to suffer through a harangue by Senator Jenner in the process.

Tomorrow the pages are all to be presented with magnificent Hawaiian shirts by the Delegate from Hawaii, Mrs. Farrington. This should be quite something.

Estes, back from somewhere, said to Senator K., "I was sorry I could not get out to your state." "So were we," replied K., smiling happily. "Tell them I love them anyway," Estes suggested.

One of the shocks of Kefauver's visit was the jolly way he and Humphrey got along. It was thought that they would not speak to one another after Kefauver bucked the Humphrey machine in Minnesota. Yet Kefauver was as unwelcome as ever to all others. When he came in to vote, his regular seat was empty but surrounded on all sides by many senators. Rather than enter the crowd, he sat down in an empty seat in a deserted section of the floor.

June 20, 1956

This is a typical example of my exhausting work schedule: On Wednesday, I came to work at 11:00 A.M. Between 12:00 and 2:00 we passed a new accounting procedure for the Federal government that is supposed to save $5 billion by eliminating unexpended balances. At 2:00 Senator Clements called me to the office to "gladhand" the four top 4-Hers from Kentucky. The Senator was busy and could not get off to show them around Washington, so he detailed me to the task. We climbed into our chauffeured black Cadillac for a three-hour jaunt around town. Senator Clements does not have a car in Washington, and so when he needs one he borrows one of the two Cadillacs of the Sergeant-at-Arms or one of the two of the Secretary of the Senate. Beside these, Cadillacs are provided for the Financial Clerk, the Attending Physician, the Secretary for the Majority, and the Majority and Minority Leaders. Well, we toured in great splendor from the Russian Embassy to Arlington Cemetery, from the National Gallery of Art to the Pentagon. I dropped off my friends on the other side of town and rode back to the Capitol in solitary splendor in the back of my black Caddy. I arrived a few minutes after the Senate had adjourned for the day, and I had the ego-stimulating thrill of arriving in style just as one of my various bosses was flagging down a cab. Come to think of it, he's practically the only boss I have who doesn't have a furnished Cadillac of his own.

The Senate lately has been in the throes of appropriations bills. For instance, last week we appropriated $14,000 for one year's maintenance of a car for the Speaker and $7,500 as salary for the janitor who sweeps the Senate floor every morning. There has also been some discussion of whether to cut $1 billion from the defense bill. In other words, things have been pretty listless. But you can generally count on Joe McCarthy to perk things up a bit.

The good Senator wobbled into the Chamber on Thursday, looking even more ghastly than usual. He was white, and I have never seen him so shaky during a speech. I was sitting about ten feet away (I returned to the Republican side of the rostrum for the occasion so as to be able to look up into his bleary eyes while he spoke), and he was shaking so that, when he laid the pages of his speech aside one by one, he never could get them on the table beside him properly, and they kept falling to the floor around him. When a page went over to pick them up, the Senator waved him away with a weak gesture, and so the sheets kept falling around his feet, adding a note of utter confusion to the impact, confounding enough in its own right, of his speech.

The Senator was, as usual, very quotable and an entrancing speaker. His heavy, slightly slurred monotone, his sneers of jolting sharpness added fascination to his dissipated alcoholic appearance. You become more or less accustomed to a profusion of niceties and rambling compliments, which sometimes end up in very involved sentences and always have a tendency to obscure what is being said after sitting in the Senate for a while. Witness the preceding sentence. McCarthy has no one to say nice things about, so his speeches are always as refreshing as a kick from Indian Charlie. He began his speech in this way:

"Mr. President, the best news that has come out of Washington in a long time was the announcement that the Supreme Court has concluded its final session of the term . . . During the past six or seven months the irresponsibility of that tribunal has sunk to unprecedented depths . . . [Its actions are] manifestly absurd and unjustifiable . . . I may say, in passing, that the Supreme Court, since the appointment of Mr. Warren, has sunk to the greatest low in its history . . . The decisions became worse and worse . . . I have learned not to underestimate the ability of the Supreme Court to come up with an even greater travesty in the future." While it doesn't greatly matter, he was talking about the decision on the security program, which declared it unlawful to fire a meat inspector for being a Communist. He promised with great solemnity that he was going to introduce legislation to "curb" the power of the Court.

There is a general tendency to assert that McCarthy is thick-skinned, that he is immune to criticism, that he has withdrawn into an impenetrable hard shell from which vantage point he spews out his venom. Concrete proof was offered during his speech. While the Senator was speaking, there alighted on his balding noggin a fly. Now, a fly is fairly unusual in Washington, and for a fly to sneak into the heavily guarded Senate chamber is an event of note. This was a large fly, and his progress was easily observable from my station a few feet away. He made several tentative reconnaissance patrols down either side of McCarthy's bald spot, but when the going got rough he returned to the relatively unobstructed zone on top, where he proceeded to turn somersaults. My gaze had shifted from the Senator's bleary eyes and wobbly stance and was riveted on the fly. For several minutes the fly tried to get a rise out of the Senator. As the minutes passed and still it received no attention, it became discouraged and finally swooped off in disgust.

Friday furnished a good example of why I much prefer working on the Democratic side to doing nothing on the Republican side. Regardless of the reasons for it and regardless of your opinion of it, the fact remains that the Democrats do, at a conservative estimate, nine-tenths of the talking in the Senate. Some of the reasons are that (1) the Democrats control the Senate and are thus responsible for committees and guiding the passage of legislation; (2) the Democrats are out of power so far as the Presidency is concerned and are thus much more outspoken in any grievances they may have. These reasons, however, cannot entirely account for the undeniably dynamic quality of the Democratic side. Intending no reflection on the relative merits of the respective parties, I think I can say dispassionately that the Democratic side contains many more colorful, aggressive and repulsive characters. Think, for instance, of all the Senators you have heard mentioned for the Presidency: Symington, Johnson, Kefauver, Kerr, Russell, Knowland. Knowland is the only Republican in the group, and the only reason for that is that he is always mentioning himself. Besides which the Democrats have Fulbright, Douglas and George. All the Republicans have is McCarthy.

This discussion is meant to be an introduction to what happened today, following Secretary Wilson's statement that Senate efforts to raise defense appropriations were "phony." A handful of major speeches were given on the subject, lasting several hours. Beside this a group of Democrats got into a gleeful exchange of caustic comments, which pulled everyone into the act on the Democratic side. It was obviously rigged to a certain extent. Stu Symington gave the lead-off speech, after which he yielded to various senators for comment. In yielding he had the careful guidance of Lyndon Johnson. Throughout all these hours of debate the only Republican utterance was a two-sentence comment by Styles Bridges, who also deplored the Wilson statement.

The moral is that I have a much better view of what goes on from the Democratic side of the rostrum, because that is where everything happens. I go back to the Republican side only to witness McCarthy's occasional exhibitions. All the Democrats have grievances or causes. Eastland rants about segregation, Morse rants about integration, Humphrey rants about everything.

June 26, 1956

This week was highlighted by a speech by my idol, Senator John Kennedy of Massachusetts, who will be Vice-President under Stevenson if Eisenhower falls down a flight of stairs and breaks his neck. I am very much impressed by it. I think it should be framed and hung on the wall of every college instructor.

[This speech of Kennedy's which so impressed me was actually not given on the Senate floor, but at the Harvard commencement exercises of June 14, 1956. It was characteristic of Kennedy to save his moments of eloquence for his public addresses around the country; in the Senate he conducted himself modestly and matter-of-factly. I was not the only person in the Senate, however, on whom this speech made an impression. It came to my attention because it was inserted in the *Record* by Lyndon Johnson, who described it as "the most eloquent defense of politics and politicians that it has ever been my pleasure to read." The speech, whose text can be found on pages 10800 to 10801 of the *Congressional Record*, 84th Congress, 2nd Session, Volume 102, Part 8, is certainly as relevant today as when it was written. It deplores the suspicion and antagonism which exists between politicians and intellectuals. The speech suggests something of the spirit of the Kennedy of this period, and why he had such an appeal to students like myself. It is also significant because one of Kennedy's major contributions to American public life was precisely in this area, building bridges between the worlds of intellect and politics.]

Here are a few excerpts from the speech:

[I]t is regrettable that the gap between the intellectual and the politician seems to be growing. Instead of synthesis, clash and discord now characterize the relations between the

130

two groups much of the time. . . . Both sides in this battle, it seems to me, are motivated by largely unfounded feelings of distrust. The politician, whose authority rests upon the mandate of the popular will, is resentful of the scholar who can, with dexterity, slip from position to position without dragging the anchor of public opinion. It was this skill that caused Lord Melbourne to say of the youthful historian Macaulay that he wished he was as sure of anything as Macaulay was of everything. The intellectual, on the other hand, finds it difficult to accept the differences between the laboratory and the legislature. In the former, the goal is truth, pure and simple, without regard to changing currents of public opinion; in the latter, compromises and majorities and procedural customs and rights affect the ultimate decision as to what is right or just or good. . . .

I would ask both groups to recall that the American politician of today and the American intellectual of today are descended from a common ancestry. Our Nation's first great politicians were also among the Nation's first great writers and scholars. . . . In those golden years, our political leaders moved from one field to another with amazing versatility and vitality . . . I would hope that both groups, recalling their common heritage, might once again forge a link between the intellectual and political professions. I know that scholars may prefer the mysteries of pure scholarship or the delights of abstract discourse. But, "Would you have counted him a friend of ancient Greece," as George William Curtis asked a century ago during the Kansas-Nebraska controversy, "who quietly discussed patriotism on that Greek summer day through whose hopeless and immortal hours Leonidas and his 300 stood at Thermopylae for liberty? Was John Milton to conjugate Greek verbs in his library or talk of the liberty of the ancient Shunamites when the liberty of Englishmen was imperiled?" No, the duty of the scholar, particularly in a republic such as ours, is to contribute his objective views and his sense of liberty to the affairs of his State and Nation. . . . We do not need scholars or politicians like Lord

131

John Russell, of whom Queen Victoria remarked, he would be a better man if he knew a third subject—but he was interested in nothing but the constitution of 1688 and himself. What we need are men who can ride easily over broad fields of knowledge and recognize the mutual dependence of our two worlds.

"Don't teach my boy poetry," an English mother recently wrote the Provost of Harrow. "Don't teach my boy poetry; he he is going to stand for Parliament." Well, perhaps she was right—but if more politicians knew poetry, and more poets knew politics, I am convinced the world would be a little better place in which to live.

The second lesson in philosophy this week came from Senator Mundt, who asserts that the Supreme Court in some way has come under the secret influence of the Communists. He lit into the Fund for the Republic on the occasion of the release of its *Report on Blacklisting*, which criticizes the practice of denying an author the courtesy of judging his script on the basis of the script itself. Now a script is judged by the political background of the author on the assumption that though the judge is too stupid to locate it himself there might be some corrupting influence in it. Mundt got off one good one—referring to the Fund as the ugly duckling hatched from a $15 million egg of the Ford Foundation.

Senator O. is a continual and unremitting sot who seldom manages to get his head above the table. For some inexplicable reason he reminds me of Raggedy Ann, who, if my information is accurate, is a rather dull doll. He looks out at the world from wide, glazed, stupefied eyes. Besides, he is shapeless all over.

Candidate Kefauver, who, in his spare time, is also a Senator, came up to me the other day and said: "Do you have a piece of gum? I've got to meet some clergymen," indicating that his breath was not what you might call presentable. I told him I didn't chew.

From time to time I have described the work of the person who really runs the Senate, Bobby Baker, Secretary for the Majority. I mentioned, for instance, that he always found out how a vote was going before it went, to avoid unpleasantness if possible. Today I was talking to him about what he will be doing at the Democratic convention. He is Clerk of the Platform Committee, and he will also poll delegations who request it on the floor. Thus he will be able to use his two chief talents for keeping everything straight and smoothing things into an even course. If you are looking for a good tip on what sort of platform the Democrats will have this year, the best indication I can give you is the fact that Bobby Baker is from South Carolina.

Capitol Hill was at a standstill for an hour last week, as the pages left their jobs (with permission) to get a look at Kim Novak. The pages were asked to form in a group behind Miss Novak by NBC-TV, and we formed the background and supplied the appreciative response. Since Kim is from Chicago, she was greeted by that master of the modulated polysyllable, Everett McKinley Dirksen. Kim was wearing her hair gray to match her dress. She arrived in three Thunderbirds, which isn't easy.

The sight in the former Supreme Court chamber (now used as a committee room) the other day was a little ludicrous. Senator Symington and his Air Force Subcommittee were grouped behind a table. Facing them was, literally, the entire defense establishment. The group was headed by Charlie Wilson and Admiral Radford, Chairman of the Joint Chiefs of Staff. Behind them sat various insignificant undersecretaries, the Secretaries of the Army, Navy and Air Force, and the Commandant of the Marine Corps and the Chiefs of Staff of the Army and Navy. The Chief of Staff of the Air Force was in Moscow; he was the only one missing. What was all this brass gathered in one place for? Well, after listening to three hours of hearings, it would be hard to say for what purpose the whole show was rigged.

Wilson started off with a statement whose message was, "All's right with the world." Then Symington and his committee set out on their task of trying to befuddle him. They set before him in rapid succession a series of documents urging economy, which he had written during the past years. They tried to confuse him by dropping the papers in his lap in rapid succession and accusing him in horrified tones of that cardinal sin, economy. As I said, this went on for three hours. After listening to Wilson for that length of time, I began to realize why he gets so much adverse publicity. It's because he likes to speak his mind, which is utterly ridiculous and foolhardy. At various points he started off on philosophical tangents, winding up with such statements as "I really think the Russians like us" and "We must not be caught in a suicidal rush for an ever bigger and better army." To this last one, Symington replied, "Then would you advocate an ever smaller and worse army?"

Major action this week (besides passing a trifling $33 billion road program) was the debate on the foreign-aid bill, which kept us in until after 11:00 P.M. on Thursday and Friday. The night sessions are always lots of fun. Senators are no longer besieged by reporters and constituents and mail, and they have a chance to relax and talk. A group of Republican senators got together to tell unsavory stories. But what interested me most was a discussion by several Democratic senators of John Foster Dulles. Senator George was doing most of the theorizing, and other senators were passing judgment on his opinions. George always talks very slowly, and, since it is so difficult for him to say anything, you get the feeling he would never bother to say anything he did not sincerely believe. He started off by saying that in his opinion the basic thing wrong with the State Department was John Dulles. He said the American people had no confidence in him. Then the senators tired to decide what was wrong with Mr. Dulles. "He's intelligent," asserted George, "but there's something about him I don't like. I think it's sort of intuition." Other senators agreed. George ended the discussion this way: "Once the President makes up his mind, he doesn't pay any attention to John."

Various results of the debate on foreign aid might be cited. Senator Symington, for instance, showed a dismaying lack of perception in his votes. The overall feeling was one of great dissatisfaction with the administration's program. Twenty-five senators voted against all foreign aid, and no one seemed satisfied with the presentation of the executive. Senator George was the most eloquent spokesman for the increase in aid, and I have already cited his opinion of Mr. Dulles.

By far the most memorable speech was that of Senator George, Chairman of the Foreign Relations Committee. It was the most moving experience I have ever had in the Senate. I actually find it very difficult to say anything appreciative about anything after having heard months of nauseating and meaningless eulogies and praise. After hearing people refer to Herman Welker as the "great and distinguished Senator from Idaho," those adjectives are very difficult for me to use; yet, truthfully, I thought George's speech was moving and eloquent. He spoke with more force than he is physically capable of. His voice cracked and broke with emotion. While I ridiculed McCarthy for not being able to hold onto his speech and letting it fall all around him, the same thing added poignancy to Senator George's speech. As he pounded on his desk, books and papers mounted around his feet; he was oblivious of them. With deep reverence Senator Mansfield moved quietly into the seat beside him to make sure that nothing more would fall on the Senator. Quite often he lost his train of thought in the middle of a sentence. He spoke in broken phrases and often referred to "these things" when he couldn't place the right word. All of this, while calling for derision in another, added great force to the impassioned plea of Senator George. I think that after his speech other senators felt as I did: that superlatives and compliments have become so commonplace that they are trite and fulsome. Not a soul said a word in commendation of the speech. They all gathered round and silently shook his hand.

His plea was basically that we should maintain the program on principle because it would be very dangerous to abandon it. He had nothing complimentary to say about the way it is being executed at present.

Speeches in opposition to the foreign-aid program were in two categories: those delivered by critical senators and those delivered by benighted senators. About the most benighted senator in existence is good old Senator Z. I never tire of listening to his endlessly inept and amusing speeches. He, of course, is against all foreign aid and always has been. He upholds his unblemished

135

record of misjudgment with ingratiating pride. He had prepared a charming speech on the foreign-aid bill. But, since an agreement had been made that general debate would be cut off and there would only be an hour spent on each amendment, he had to introduce an amendment to be able to make his speech. The amendment he devised was such a monstrosity that it gave all the senators a good laugh. The Senator blushed with modesty at the half-stifled chuckles around him as his amendment was read. It specified that there would be no more foreign aid until the exemption for dependents on the Federal income tax was raised to $700. Of course this amendment has nothing to do with foreign aid, but Senator Z. will have nothing to do with it either. Well, it gave him his chance to make his important speech. Since I have cultivated a great fascination for the unerring miscalculation of this great patriot, I had already read his speech and so was able to reap just that much more pleasure from his wholly inadequate delivery.

"Certainly, if I had politics in mind regarding foreign-aid programs, I would have been supporting them years ago when they were popular," declaimed my oak-headed friend. With the dexterity of a three-legged rhinoceros he plunged to the heart of the problem. "The one-world theorists are firmly entrenched, and our only weapon to curtail their subtle program of amalgamating America with the rest of the world is to cut off their money. These people I speak of in the State Department and elsewhere want to do away with every conceivable difference between us and the rest of the world. For years they have been working like beavers tearing down trade protection barriers, immigration walls, money exchanges and the like until it's now easier for a foreign government to contact and get assistance from Washington than it is for an American citizen." He took the textile industry as an example of what was happening. "Last week, one of the most terrible examples of misuse of authority I have ever heard of took place. I have it on unimpeachable authority that representatives of American textile industry appearing before this American (Tariff) Commission for relief to save jobs of American workers and American industry, were subjected to cross-examination by representatives of a foreign government. . . . To me, the fact that foreign government representatives were even allowed to cross-examine Americans before an American commission is revolting and represents the degeneration that has taken place in bureaucratic government. It points up the need for Congress to personally take up this matter and to obstruct any such future situations by halting all this foreign aid." To add to the fun, the Senator missed a couple of pages and skipped right into the middle of a totally disconnected sentence a couple of pages farther on, to his great wonderment and our amusement.

But there were many senators who were conscientiously disturbed about the administration of the foreign-aid program. Senator Ellender, for instance, has been around the world four times and displayed menacingly on the floor his journal (fully a foot thick) of those trips. He found complete English libraries in the middle of the Belgian Congo, technical plants and planes given to natives who hadn't the faintest notion what to do with them and so on for several hours.

Today's history lesson: When Eastland was being elected Chairman of the Judiciary Committee there was a fight to take it away from him. Barkley said that if it succeeded it would be the third time in history. The other two: In 1923 Senator Cummins was bypassed, and the chairmanship of the Interstate Commerce Committee was given to someone else. The reason given in this case was that Cummins was already Senate President Pro Tempore, but it still took 23 roll-call votes to resolve the issue. In 1925 Senator Edwin Ladd, Republican from North Dakota, was denied the chairmanship of the Public Lands Committee; it was given to Senator Robert Stanfield, a Republican from Oregon. Ladd was one of about eight Republicans in the Senate who were very progressive, remnants of the old Bull Moose Party. Because the Democrats abstained from voting, the Old Guard had a majority, and he was dumped because he was charged with not being a true Republican. Ladd was so crushed that he died a few months later. The Senate Parliamentarian who had been here since 1916 and knows everything is my source.

137

July 12, 1956

I guess there is no more pertinent authority on the subject of adjournment than the Majority Leader. Here is what that august gentleman had to say: "You know I'm trying to get you out of here by the 21st. . . . If we get these two money bills and the Social Security out of the way I'm ready to say good-bye."

To meet this goal, the pages are being pushed to the utmost. While before I have rarely batted an eye before 9:30 in the morning, the pages must now start working at the incredible hour of 9:00 A.M. because we are starting sessions early in the morning and working until about 6:00 or 7:00 or 8:00 every night. Fortunately the terrible strain of being at work at such an ungodly hour of the morning will not last long.

On my rounds this week I had the glorious opportunity of making the acquaintance (more fully) of Senator O. When I sauntered into his office, in place of a desk filled with important matters presently before the Senate, instead of a countenance furrowed with plans for the betterment of the nation, I found the distinguished Senator facing an empty desk on which he had spread his mid-afternoon snack. He finished off his coke and sandwich as we talked.

Some other unpleasantries: In 1952 the Republican Policy Committee publicized the analysis of a handwriting expert, who said that from his signature Eisenhower appeared to be aggressive and forthright. When the same handwriting expert this year said that Ike's signature showed definite signs of fatigue and rundown condition, however, no such treatment was accorded his views. In connection with this, I scrutinized some of the multitudinous Eisenhower signatures which come to the Senate on nominations and so forth. I found the signature shapeless and completely devoid of character; the overall downward slant of the signature, with an especially weak, slanting finishing flourish, seemed to reveal the complete incompetence of the President.

Naturally it was preposterous to countenance having a session on the day of the All-Star Game between the American and National Leagues, so, while all the senators were (I hope) yelling themselves hoarse at the game downtown, the House of Representatives and I kept the wheels of government careening drunkenly along. I had never attended a meeting of the fabled House Unamerican Activities Committee, where the ferocious representative Francis Walter has his den, and when they started making rumbling noises about blacklisting I raced right over. The issue was the recently published report of John Cogley, former editor of *Commonweal*, on blacklisting in the entertainment industry, which had already been attacked by Senator Mundt as I have reported.

The Committee puts on a wonderful show, and this was one of the best hearings I have attended. The counsel, Richard Arens, is a real ham. Most of the Capitol counsels sit at a desk and ask questions; Mr. Arens stomps around gesturing dramatically and emotes questions. It is very effective when he turns his back on the witness and asks questions of the wall, shrugging in exasperation.

The hearing immediately struck a discordant note. Originally it was to be a closed meeting, and Mr. Cogley was not told that the press would be present until two minutes before the hearing began. One member of the press said to him that this was typical of the Committee. Perhaps this incident added to the nervousness of the witness at first.

The counsel asked Cogley about the background of the various investigators who had helped to compile the report. With great horror contorting his face, he queried, "Did you know at the time you hired him that Michael Harrington was a *socialist?*" Mr. Cogley said "yes."

Dashing forward the counsel said, "Did you know at the time you hired him that A. was for a few months twenty-two years ago a member of the Young Communist League?" Mr. Cogley said "yes." When the counsel had utilized all the shocking possibilities of these revelations, the basic issue became apparent. It was a long time coming, however, because the counsel had to qualify everything he said with great and often affected exactitude. That issue was whether blacklisting was good or bad. There never was any question as to the accuracy of the assertion in the *Report*

139

that blacklisting actually exists, because the Committee itself makes available lists of people who have been called Communists by somebody or other. So the statement of Francis Walter to the press that there is no black list, in the sense of a mimeographed form distributed around the industry was so much arrogant obscurantism. I never felt throughout the over three hours of the hearing that there was any doubt in anyone's mind that blacklisting (used in *Report* rather loosely to cover an area of discrimination) exists. Conflict came out of differing views of the validity of this process.

The counsel, for example, read from the *Report* that some actress was unable to find work because her husband pleaded the Fifth Amendment before the Unamerican Activities Committee. Mr. Cogley used this story as an illustration of the sort of unfounded blacklisting that he was trying to expose. Mr. Cogley's stand was "This is blacklisting; this is bad." "But do you realize," expounded the counsel, his extended finger quivering dramatically, "that five years later a dozen people called her a Communist before this committee?" Mr. Cogley said "yes." He managed to overcome his nervousness and take the initiative on this point. He said that what happened five years after her expulsion from decent society did not justify that expulsion. This answer evidently did not please Counsel Arens. He saw nothing wrong with blacklisting Miss L. After all, five years later someone called her a Communist. The counsel's stand was "This is blacklisting; this is good." "Why did you not put in your book the fact that this person called her a Communist five years later?" screamed the counsel, rising to a triumphant crescendo. Mr. Cogley quietly replied that there were six hundred ways in which he could have written the book. He reiterated that this had nothing whatever to do with the validity of his example.

One important issue was raised by the fact that there was a hearing at all. The very fact that Cogley was subpoenaed challenged an author's right to speak his mind without fear of being dragged up before a congressional committee to justify his opinions. Again and again during the hearing the counsel asked accusingly why this or that was not included in the book, to which

Cogley simply replied that he had not written his book in that fashion. As I said, the hearing was great fun. Arens rushed around frantically in all directions pacing the floor with affectation. Cogley was very nervous at first and merely answered the slanted questions in a defensive way, while I hoped on many occasions that he would go further and point out the real issue in question. He got better as things progressed, and he began to speak his mind more freely.

July 13, 1956

Monday was the day set aside for eulogies for late senators. Senator R. carried on an interesting discussion of the fish he had caught the day before, then came out on the floor to weep bitter tears about the aching void in his heart.

Here is a sample bit of oratory: "Mr. President, the melancholy truth of the aphorism that death loves a shining mark was distressingly attested on the 28th day of last February when the monarch of human destroyers ended the earthly career of the eminent Senator Harley Kilgore. . . . It caused sorrow . . . in the hearts of more than a million West Virginia men and women who considered him not only their peerless friend but also the guardian of their liberty, the champion of their rights, and the defender of the faith. . . . It seems but yesterday that he was with us in the full strength of manhood, endowed with joyous life, and peace and sweet content and as happy as fancy ever feigned. Now we call his name in vain. His lifeless lips are as silent as the tomb. This faithful friend will nevermore be seen through the illusions of love, the telescopes of science or the tears of grief."

As usual Senator Z. carried off the honors as the most inept and the most intriguing speaker. He read John Donne's piece about no man being an island, and by the time he got down to for whom the bell was tolling he had lost his place a couple of times, got screwed up, put in a "not" somewhere that ruined the entire sentence and in general made a riot of the whole thing. His best blun-

141

der, however, was when he struck out on his own, leaving out a pertinent syllable in the following phrase, "Senator N. and his inmate friends."

On Sunday I went to see the Yankees slaughter the Washington Senators. Washington put on a convincing demonstration of why it is somewhere around the bottom of the league. We sat in center field so that we could see the muscles rippling in Mickey Mantle's back and hurl disparaging epithets at him.

Charlie Wilson returned to the congressional wars on Monday and found that Democratic senators had been nursing their grievances over the weekend and were really ready to let loose. Again he brought the whole Pentagon with him: all the secretaries and undersecretaries and the whole Joint Chiefs of Staff. Indeed the very fact that the Committee was honored by so many celebrities gave rise to an unpleasant comment in the charged atmosphere. Senator Jackson asked bluntly, to start the questioning: "Don't the Joint Chiefs have anything to do? We didn't ask them to come."

At another point, while Wilson was groping for an answer, Chairman Symington said, "Of course, if you feel that you are not capable of answering the question . . ." When Wilson asked Senator Jackson to read again, "what you thought General Twining said," Symington chimed in coldly with, "This is not what Senator Jackson *thinks* General Twining said; this is his actual statement."

The star of the show was Senator Ervin of North Carolina, who belongs to the old school of politicians. He never asks a question without seizing the opportunity to tell a story. He prefaced his questions by saying that, now that he had been reconstructed once, he did not want to be reconstructed by the Russians. When Wilson said he thought our forces would do a wonderful job in any war, Ervin said, "Well, all those people at the Alamo did a wonderful job too, but it didn't do 'em much good." Then he got started on the emphasis on economy under the Wilson regime. He said he thought that the Pentagon was obsessed with this one theme. This, quite naturally, reminded him of a story, of the Baptist preacher who always talked on immersion. After he had preached on the subject for a year, the board of deacons per-

142

suaded him to preach on a text they would select for him, hoping to get him on another subject. The text they chose was "In the beginning, God created the heavens and the earth." The preacher said, "The composition of the earth is one-third land and two-thirds water, which brings me to my subject, which is baptism by immersion." Ervin ended by saying that he thought the Defense Department was also stuck on one word, "economy." He suggested that in matters of national defense it might be wise to do a little more immersing and a little less sprinkling.

I have now sat and looked at the Secretary of Defense for six hours, on Friday and Monday. On the whole he acquitted himself well, though he made no attempt to move from his defensive position; he let the Democrats carry the fight to him. He was calm, almost, but not quite, grim. He also at times seemed to be woefully uninformed and was always trying to refer a question to one of his inferiors. But the chief recollection I have of him is his perhaps fatal love of philosophizing and rambling, a love that has caused him endless embarrassment. To many questions by Senator Jackson, Wilson never gave what you could call an answer. He would always be prompted to clarify some aspect of the problem raised in the query and would never really attack the specific issue until Jackson growlingly dragged him back by the scruff of the neck. (On Tuesday, Wilson asked Jackson to his face for an apology for his disrespectful behavior.) At one point he said it was too bad the czars were no longer around somewhere for the Russians to hate, so that they would not hate Americans. When Senator Ervin finished the story I have repeated, instead of addressing himself to the question of economy, Wilson recalled that he himself had been baptized by immersion in the Something-or-other River. I didn't go back on Tuesday and therefore missed Wilson's remark about the mama whale who told junior that you only get harpooned when you're spouting off.

Some unpleasant facts I have dug up this week: I saw a directive stating that all the Democratic senators were to be invited to a banquet for Senator George, all that is except poor Senator Kefauver. It is really pathetic to see this guy wandering around the

Senate. He hasn't a friend in the world, or at least in the senatorial world. He seems reluctant to debate with anybody on the floor and gives the impression of being apprehensive that the other senators may not be courteous to him. Beside the small core of his office force, who tenaciously idolize him, not a soul has a kind word for him. Not that he deserves anything but pity. He is very close to being the least effective senator around.

July 20, 1956

That great champion of nothing, Senator O., has been consistently maintaining his high and unblemished record of inadequacy. He spent this week on the floor reading two paperbacks entitled *Storm Fear* and *The Killers*. I thought there might be some hope for his literary taste when I caught the title of the latter, but it had no connection with the Hemingway version. I have decided that the main duties of his administrative assistant are to make sure that the boss is liberally supplied with suitable reading material.

But I doubt that even the gripping realism of *Storm Fear* could equal that of the past week on the Senate floor. We have been working fifteen hours a day, and this is our first six-day week. Major legislation has been whizzing past at breakneck speed. Rushing past like St. Vitus being chased by a bulldog were social security, Hell's Canyon, mutual security, Paul Hoffman for United Nation delegate and a well-lobbied executive pay-raise bill. Then even such a minor bill as the Customs Simplification Act was able to stir up scintillating discussion of free trade versus protective tariffs. Senator Pastore of Rhode Island, the champion of New England industrialism, proved again that no one can top him in open debate and that, although he may be only five feet tall, five feet of burning wrath can consume the entire chamber in a burst of fiery sarcasm. Then we had jewels of oratory ranging from vicious Senator J., through Senator V. sighing like a wet cow, to the enraptured, inspiring tones of the master of superfluity, Everett Dirksen.

I can give only the most tattered account of all these awe-inspir-

144

ing events. For the past week the Democrats have been run ragged with preparations for the Walter George Appreciation Dinner ($100 a plate). Such slight complications as the fact that the estimated attendance of five hundred was exceeded by one thousand did not serve to lighten the burden.

Bobby Baker and his staff assumed a large share of the control of the planning. He kept the $150,000 in his office. He plotted where those extra thousand people were to sit, staying up until 2:00 A.M. and 4:00 A.M. respectively the nights before the event. Everyone seems to have found something to do. I dashed downtown to pick up the tickets and placecards. When I got back, I had to rush off again to have the gift to be presented to Mrs. George properly wrapped downtown.

The trouble with planning something like this for all the most important people in the Democratic Party of the country is that there are always a large number of people who think they are important enough to wait until the last minute to make their arrangements. So on the day of the dinner Lyndon Johnson decrees that he doesn't care who has to be shoved back in order to get Mr. Somebody who really is Somebody at the head table. Then Joseph Clark (a bigwig from Philadelphia)[4] phoned to give Bobby Baker the word that he had decided that he would be able to be present at the head table after all. Naturally there were people who went away in a huff, such as Senator W., who said he wasn't going to stand for the good people of his state being put in the back of the room. Baker's office was besieged with calls all day from all 1,500 people wanting to know where they were going to sit.

Several of the pages from Georgia went to the banquet. In their minds the outstanding feature of the event was Adlai Stevenson's remark that he felt like a mosquito in a nudist colony: He didn't know where to start.

I had a talk with my idol Senator Kennedy the other day. I told him I was going to be a freshman at Harvard in the fall. He says four Kennedy brothers have graduated from Harvard. He says if I feel in the mood to donate my services to the Democratic Party of Massachusetts he will see to it that I meet the Right People.

Note to the George dinner: One Republican senator who is run-

[4] At that time he had not yet become Senator Joseph Clark.

145

ning for re-election this year was all set to buy up a table for ten ($1,000) for the George dinner when he found out that the proceeds are going to the Democratic Senatorial Campaign Committee.

One memorable speech on foreign aid, which I forgot to mention, was that given by Russell Long, opposing all aid. Russell's father and mother both served in the Senate, and his uncle is Governor Earle Long of Louisiana. His father Huey's statue is prominent in the Capitol. Russell was elected to the Senate six years ago at the age of 29 (since a senator must be 30, he had to wait awhile before he could take office officially) and after six years in the Senate is still the youngest member. It isn't often that Russell shows that he belongs to the Long family. He spends most of his time trotting around looking almost as smug and self-satisfied as Dick Nixon (to whom he bears a resemblance). But when you come to foreign affairs, you are striking close to the family tradition. He recently carried off the coveted honor of a post on the Foreign Relations Committee, replacing Senator Barkley, where he will be able to carry on his crusade against the Communist warlords, the British warlords, the French warlords, the German warlords, the . . . but I think you get the idea. At times when he is faced with the prospect of sending money to such despicable bastards, he can wax wonderfully eloquent. His speech was a real classic, and there was a lot of good meaty stuff in it. What brought down the house was his anguished cry that we are sending money to Tito but we don't have anything for dear old Granny.

Fortunately I do not have to work sixteen hours a day six days a week. There are enough summer additions to the page corps to make a somewhat modified shift system workable. Some days I come to work at 5:00 P.M. and work all night. Other days I come when the Senate convenes at 9:00 A.M. or so and leave in the evening. This makes for a rather uneven view of Senate activities.

I was present, however, for every excited syllable of the debate on the nomination of Paul Hoffman. It was highlighted by an address by Senator Flanders refuting McCarthy. Senator Flanders is a Vermonter who looks perpetually asleep. A moustache makes it appear that his nose is dragging on his chin, and his chin is dragging on his chest. This strange bald creature goes around looking Rip Van Winklish and spreading good cheer. He is really very sweet and hilariously self-effacing. When Senator Q. rushed up to him and said: "Where have you been keeping yourself? I wish I saw more of you," Flanders said, "Well, of course there are two sides to that." Today Flanders crawled out of the cave, yawned, climbed into his 1920 suit and told McCarthy to mind his own business.

Senator McCarthy was in rare form: sober form. He seemed to be rather less drunk than usual. His speech was very powerful, and more than on many occasions he displayed that latent power that rests in his bull neck, his ferocious eyebrows and his slurring monotone. Deadly, deliberate, ominous, with the slow, compelling momentum of a steam roller: That's our Joe.

While Joe was stalking his prey with silent stealth, Senator V. was using the more exciting, just as chilling "You don't scare me you betcha" approach of a rather overconfident rattlesnake. While Joe was content to approach the petrified rabbit quietly, almost gingerly, Senator J. was displaying tactics more calculated to raise hares than to transform them into a shuddering stuttering state of terror. Jutting his jaw, hunching his head forward on his shoulders with lethal determination, flailing his arms like a drunken channel swimmer, he was off in hot pursuit. He was biting, snapping and snarling, dashing in angrily where Joe likes to tread silently behind the curtain.

Tuesday, July 24, 1956

The last two days have been the tensest of the session. On Monday the House passed the administration civil-rights program and sent it to the Senate. One of the House clerks comes to the door of the chamber, is announced and presents his message. The House clerk stood outside the chamber for a full ten minutes while things were arranged inside. First, Senator Lister Hill of Alabama took the presiding officer's chair. Presiding is a chore that is generally

147

relegated to the most junior senators, for the Parliamentarian can always tell them what to say. When one of the younger senators, William Laird of West Virginia, unwittingly offered to relieve him, Hill graciously declined. Then Lyndon Johnson made very sure that there were no radical liberals in the chamber at the moment. Paul Douglas had gone over to the House chamber to find out what had happened to the bill; some others were engaged in a conversation in the cloakroom. At the prescribed instant, the House clerk entered the chamber and rattled off his message, and in five seconds Lister Hill had referred it to Eastland's Judiciary Committee. When Paul Douglas raced back from the other side of the Capitol just too late, he complained to the presiding officer of such supersonic speed, commenting that no bill was ever sent to the other chamber for at least a couple of hours.

Then the furor was on in full swing. You could tell it by the way senators were going around in small groups, not even giving civil nods to others—and by the way that everyone under questioning had a strange degree of ignorance on the subject. I asked Senator MacNamara what he thought was going to happen, and he laughed off my question uneasily. Liberal Hubert Humphrey had a huddle with Lyndon Johnson, who, while keeping mum on his position on civil rights, is siding with the Southerners in an attempt to end the session without a filibuster. Lyndon Johnson dragged out a copy of the Senate rules and showed the doubting Hubert that the referral to Eastland's committee had been legal. He also made it clear that he had all the angles figured, because he outlined what he would have done had some liberal objected; he had his statement all ready backing up the referral to committee. He was able to avoid this by sneaking in the bill behind their backs. He ended up his lecture to Humphrey by saying, "This is probably the most important lesson you'll learn in the Senate—to look at the rules."

Well, battle had been declared. As usual the Republicans sat around as spectators while the Democrats had it out. All major legislation, all debate, everything happens on the Democratic side of the aisle. Three Democrats vowed that they would attempt to pull on others just as mean a trick as had been done unto them: Paul Douglas of Illinois, Herbert Lehman of New York and

Thomas Hennings of Missouri. They are dedicated to bringing up the civil-rights bill at all costs. The reasons for this determination to risk a filibuster are various. Senator M. said he thought Douglas was the only one of the lot who was sincere. The other two senators are up for re-election, Lehman in minority-conscious New York and Hennings in Missouri. Hennings said that if they didn't pass some sort of civil-rights legislation it would mean his defeat because of the seventy thousand Negro votes in St. Louis. Whatever the reason, their ire was fired. These three Democrats vowed to offer a resolution to discharge the Committee from further consideration of the bill, thus laying it open for floor consideration. Without unanimous consent such a request can only be made in the morning hour, a period of two hours at the beginning of each session following adjournment. And so for the past couple of days the Senate has been recessing rather than adjourning, so that the Douglas motion cannot be made because there is always some Southerner on hand to object.

The liberals have counterattacked. Without a morning hour, minor bills and uncontroversial matters cannot be considered without unanimous consent. So the liberal three have taken it upon themselves to object to the routine requests of everyone else, trying to force the calling of a morning hour. Even requests for having editorials and statements printed in the *Record*, of which there are dozens every day, were objected to. Only one such request for the printing of a statement slipped by, and Senator Lehman apologized later for having been "asleep at the switch."

Johnson made it very clear that he considered this struggle a test of his leadership. He warned the senators against going against their leadership.

In an effort to get an adjournment, Douglas moved that the Senate adjourn for five minutes. This motion was defeated on a roll-call vote. This is the first instance of open warfare on the Senate floor that I have witnessed. It is the first time one group of senators has refused even to trust another. The liberals have every right not to trust the leadership after the way they have been treated. I have never seen a case in which a senator interested in a piece of legislation was not notified of its consideration. I have

149

never seen such a deliberate attempt to pull a fast one on a bill. Of course it is easy to sympathize with Johnson's exasperation in his attempts to complete the session, but it is hard to condone the limits to which he has gone. He has lost the confidence of certain members of his party. Normally any request by the Majority Leader is immediately granted, and no one even pays any attention to it. Today Lehman was rushing down from the back of the chamber objecting right and left whenever Johnson opened his mouth for even the most insignificant announcement. Always before the opposing factions on an issue have had it understood that both sides would be fully cognizant of every formal motion of the opposition. There has never been such an insinuation of underhandedness or such bitter personal antagonism between factions.

While all this was embroiling just about everyone else, Senator O. finished the seduction scene in Chapter 16 and plunged into Chapter 17 of *The Killers*.

Thursday, July 26, 1956

Well, on Wednesday the whole controversy had passed over. Douglas is too gracious and understanding a person to stay in an irritated, obstructive frame of mind for very long. When he rose on Wednesday to speak on another matter he said: "It is unfortunate that I find it necessary to rise again so soon after the unpleasantness of the past few days. But I am reminded of an old Scottish saying which goes something like this: 'I lay me down to sleep each night, only to rise and bleed again.'" When Douglas starts quoting old sayings, you can be sure he is enjoying himself.

A general discussion took place in the cloakroom the other day between those who held that Stassen was an ass and those who contended that he was only a pigheaded fool, following his announcement of a campaign to refuse Nixon a second term as Vice-President. The tone of both sides was that of indulgent misanthropy or of George III dropping a comment on Benedict Arnold.

Late evening sessions really give the pages a workout. Take, for instance, Wednesday night when we had a roll-call vote at about 10:30 P.M. It just so happened that the particular vote eventually was won by the Democrats because Nixon could not be found to break a tie, so you can see how important each vote was thought to be. We were given orders to drag in every single senator, and we really had quite a time of it. Senator O., with his customary perspicacity, had wandered off and tucked himself cozily into bed without letting anyone know or asking whether there would be a vote. A phone call roused him, and one of the boys drove over wildly to pick him up while he dressed. A real problem was offered by Senator Y., who was in a besotted condition in the dining room of the Statler Hotel when we finally located him by phone. He said simply that he was not coming back. We were placed in the rather unusual position of pleading with his better nature to come back. We were finally successful in bringing these two senators to the floor in time after races across town, with the gratifying result that, as I said, we won by the margin of Nixon's absence.

Saturday, July 28, 1956

The last night of the Senate session is traditionally the most exciting of the year. Reputedly it was worth hanging around for the whole session just to be there for the wind up. There was great speculation about the time of adjournment. Some veterans confidently predicted that it would be three months after the scheduled deadline. Signs were carefully observed. When Lyndon Johnson asked the Parliamentarian to prepare certain papers necessary for adjournment, note was duly taken. When public pronouncements were made by the leaders of House and Senate, they were given grave if skeptical consideration. Then came the clincher: The disbursing office was requested to remain open until the conclusion of Senate business, an annual ritual foreboding imminent adjournment. When this warning signal was hoisted, preparations began in earnest. Those treasured bottles were triumphantly unearthed and borne aloft like tribal fetishes. As usual things happened faster among the congressmen who had less dignity to lose

151

and for once were glad of it. So we hastened first over to the House chamber.

The warm-up, hair-loosening session was in progress. This part of the ritual consisted of group singing. While Father Sam was away doing dignified things, the children played. Coya Knutson, that luscious blond, added her charming abandon to the frolic. While everyone was having a good time in this songfest, it was well understood that this was only the beginning. Some of the other pages fondly recalled past exploits that they calmly expected to be equaled before the evening was over. For instance, one of the congressmen is a retired auctioneer, and he started up a spirited round of bidding on the Capitol dome. Then there was the young congresswoman who entertained the chamber with glimpses from the routine associated with her previous occupation.

Things were getting lined up for the evening. The gentleman from W., the one with pomaded hair and that awful white suit, was getting ready for a performance at the back of the rostrum. He had been at one time a magician and had campaigned by pulling a wilted rose out of his handkerchief and saying that was the way things had been under the Republicans, then pulling out a gorgeous full-blown rose and promising that this was the way things would be when he was elected. Then Somber Sam marched back in and gaveled the House to order again to transact a little business. He, however, in his crass tyranny deliberately refrained from recognizing one commendably drunk gentleman, who was all set to offer a motion to raise the salaries of the pages. So the party came temporarily to a halt just as things were looking up. I hurried back to the Senate to check up on progress over there.

Notoriously senators consider themselves august and distinguished and that larger personification of themselves, the Senate, the world's greatest deliberative body. This attitude entails great hauteur in public, for which they compensate in private. The scene on the floor was the predictable one of various predictable senators showing satisfaction, revulsion, concern and pleasure in a sadly predictable fashion. Things were more lively in the cloakroom. Senator H. called up to say that he was checking out for the evening. Just to be exact, I said "This is Senator H., isn't it?" "No," replied Senator H., "I'm Senator N." Then he started reminiscing about his only piece of major legislation for that session, getting a postmaster for his home town. He left after getting that through on the last night, very much in need of the support that his alter ego, Senator N., was not in much condition to furnish. Senator Kefauver came over and moaned about how ghastly he felt. With due deference a page commiserated. The Senator replied considerately, hoping that the page did not feel as bad as he. "Well, Senator," replied the page, "I don't think I have quite as much liquor in me as you do." "I certainly hope not," answered the Senator.

And so it went, everyone remarking all the while that this one couldn't measure up to previous adjournments.

But I couldn't complain.

Biographical Notes

The following alphabetical listing of some of the prominent people mentioned in the *Diary* indicates the more important offices they have held before, during and after 1956.

ANDERSON, CLINTON P.: b. 1895; U.S. Secretary of Agriculture, 1945–1948; U.S. Senator (Dem.) from New Mexico, 1949–.

BAKER, ROBERT G. ("Bobby"): b. 1928; Secretary for the Senate Democratic Majority, 1955–1963.

BARKLEY, ALBEN W.: b. 1877, d. 1956; member, House of Representatives, 1913–1927; U.S. Senator (Dem.) from Kentucky, 1927–1949, 1955–1956; Senate Majority Leader, 1937–1947; Vice-President of U.S., 1949–1953.

BOWLES, CHESTER: b. 1901; Governor of Connecticut, 1949–1951; Ambassador to India and Nepal, 1951–1953; Under Secretary of State, 1961; President Kennedy's special representative for Asian, African and Latin American affairs, 1961–1963; Ambassador to India, 1963–.

BRICKER, JOHN W.: b. 1893; Governor of Ohio, 1939–1945; Republican candidate for Vice-President of U.S., 1944; U.S. Senator (Rep.) from Ohio, 1947–1958.

BRIDGES, H. STYLES: b. 1898, d. 1961; Governor of New Hampshire, 1934–1936; U.S. Senator (Rep.) from New Hampshire, 1937–1961.

CAPEHART, HOMER E.: b. 1897; U.S. Senator (Rep.) from Indiana, 1945–1963.

155

CASE, FRANCIS H.: b. 1896, d. 1962; member, House of Representatives, 1937–1951; U.S. Senator (Rep.) from South Dakota, 1951–1962.
CLEMENTS, EARLE C.: b. 1896; member, House of Representatives, 1945–1947; Governor of Kentucky, 1947–1950; U.S. Senator (Dem.) from Kentucky, 1950–1957; assistant Majority Leader, 1955–1957.
COOPER, JOHN SHERMAN: b. 1901; U.S. Senator (Rep.) from Kentucky, 1946–1949, 1952–1955, 1957–; Ambassador to India and Nepal, 1955–1956.
DANIEL, PRICE: b. 1910; attorney-general of Texas, 1946–1953; U.S. Senator (Dem.) from Texas, 1953–1956; Governor of Texas, 1956–1963.
DIRKSEN, EVERETT MCKINLEY: b. 1896; U.S. Senator (Rep.) from Illinois, 1951–; assistant Minority Leader, 1957–1959; Minority Leader, 1959–.
DOUGLAS, PAUL H.: b. 1892; U.S. Senator (Dem.) from Illinois, 1949–1967.
DULLES, JOHN FOSTER: b. 1888, d. 1959; U.S. Secretary of State, 1953–1959.
EASTLAND, JAMES O.: b. 1904; U.S. Senator (Dem.) from Mississippi, 1941, 1943–; Chairman, Senate Committee on Judiciary, 1956–.
EDEN, ANTHONY (First Earl of Avon): b. 1897; British Secretary of State for Foreign Affairs, 1935–1938, 1942–1945, 1951–1955; deputy Prime Minister, 1951–1955; Prime Minister, 1955–1957.
FULBRIGHT, J. WILLIAM: b. 1905; President, University of Arkansas, 1939–1941; U.S. Senator (Dem.) from Arkansas, 1945–; currently Chairman, Senate Committee on Foreign Relations.
GEORGE, WALTER F.: b. 1878, d. 1957; U.S. Senator (Dem.) from Georgia, 1922–1957; Chairman, Senate Committee on Foreign Relations, 1955–1957; Senate President pro tempore, 1955–1957.
GOLDWATER, BARRY: b. 1909; U.S. Senator (Rep.) from Arizona, 1953–1964; Republican candidate for President of U.S., 1964.
HARRIMAN, W. AVERELL: b. 1891; Ambassador to Russia, 1943–1946; Ambassador to Great Britain, April–October, 1946; U.S. Secretary of Commerce, 1946–1948; Governor of New York, 1955–1958; Ambassador at large, 1961, 1965–; assistant Secretary of State for Far Eastern Affairs, 1961–1963; Under Secretary of State, Political Affairs, 1963–1965.
HENNINGS, THOMAS C., JR.: b. 1903, d. 1960; member, House of Representatives, 1935–1940; U.S. Senator (Dem.) from Missouri, 1951–1960.
HUMPHREY, HUBERT H.: b. 1911; mayor of Minneapolis, 1945–1948; U.S. Senator (Dem.) from Minnesota, 1949–1965; assistant Majority Leader, 1961–1965; Vice-President of U.S., 1965–.
JOHNSON, LYNDON B.: b. 1908; member, House of Representatives, 1937–1948; U.S. Senator (Dem.) from Texas, 1949–1961; Senate

Minority Leader, 1953–1955; Majority Leader, 1955–1961; Vice-President of U.S., 1961–1963; President of U.S., 1963–.

KEFAUVER, ESTES: b. 1903, d. 1963; member, House of Representatives, 1939–1949; U.S. Senator (Dem.) from Tennessee, 1949–1963; Democratic candidate for Vice-President of U.S., 1956.

KENNEDY, JOHN F.: b. 1917, d. 1963; member, House of Representatives, 1947–1953; U.S. Senator (Dem.) from Massachusetts, 1953–1960; President of U.S., 1961–1963.

KENNEDY, ROBERT F.: b. 1925; assistant counsel, Senate permanent subcommittee on investigations, 1953; chief counsel to subcommittee minority, 1954; chief counsel and staff director of subcommittee, 1955; chief counsel, Senate Select Committee on Improper Activities in the Labor and Management Field, 1957–1960; Presidential campaign manager for John F. Kennedy, 1960; Attorney General of U.S., 1961–1964; U.S. Senator (Dem.) from New York, 1965–.

KERR, ROBERT S.: b. 1896, d. 1963; Governor of Oklahoma, 1943–1947; U.S. Senator (Dem.) from Oklahoma, 1949–1963.

KNOWLAND, WILLIAM F.: b. 1908; U.S. Senator (Rep.) from California, 1945–1958; Senate Majority Leader, 1953–1954; Minority Leader, 1955–1958.

LEHMAN, HERBERT H.: b. 1878, d. 1963; Governor of New York, 1933–1942; U.S. Senator (Dem.) from New York, 1949–1957.

LONG, RUSSELL B.: b. 1918; U.S. Senator (Dem.) from Louisiana, 1948–; assistant Majority Leader, 1965–.

MANSFIELD, MIKE: b. 1903; Professor, Montana State University, 1933–1942; member, House of Representatives, 1943–1952; U.S. Senator (Dem.) from Montana, 1953–; assistant Majority Leader, 1957–1961; Majority Leader, 1961–.

MCCARTHY, JOSEPH R.: b. 1908, d. 1957; U.S. Senator (Rep.) from Wisconsin, 1947–1957.

MCCLELLAN, JOHN L.: b. 1896; U.S. Senator (Dem.) from Arkansas, 1943–.

MINTON, SHERMAN: b. 1890, d. 1965; U.S. Senator (Dem.) from Indiana, 1935–1941; Associate Justice, U.S. Supreme Court, 1949–1956.

MORSE, WAYNE: b. 1900; Dean and Professor of Law, University of Oregon, 1931–1944; U.S. Senator (Rep.; then Independent; then Dem.) from Oregon, 1945–.

NEUBERGER, RICHARD L.: b. 1912, d. 1960; U.S. Senator (Dem.) from Oregon, 1955–1960; succeeded by his wife, Maurine B., U.S. Senator (Dem.) from Oregon, 1961–1967.

NIXON, RICHARD M.: b. 1913; U.S. Senator (Rep.) from California, 1951–1953; Vice-President of U.S., 1953–1961; Republican candidate for President of U.S., 1960.

157

PASTORE, JOHN O.: b. 1907; Governor of Rhode Island, 1945–1950; U.S. Senator (Dem.) from Rhode Island, 1950–.

RAYBURN, SAM: b. 1882, d. 1961; member, House of Representatives, 1913–1961; Speaker of the House, 1940–1961.

RUSSELL, RICHARD B.: b. 1897; Governor of Georgia, 1931–1933; U.S. Senator (Dem.) from Georgia, 1933–; Chairman, Senate Armed Services Committee.

SMITH, MARGARET CHASE: b. 1897; member, House of Representatives, 1940–1949; U.S. Senator (Rep.) from Maine, 1949–.

SPARKMAN, JOHN J.: b. 1899; member, House of Representatives, 1937–1947; U.S. Senator (Dem.) from Alabama, 1947–; Democratic candidate for Vice-President, 1952.

STEVENSON, ADLAI E.: b. 1900, d. 1965; Governor of Illinois, 1949–1953; Democratic candidate for President of U.S., 1952, 1956; U.S. Representative to the United Nations, 1961–1965.

SYMINGTON, STUART: b. 1901; assistant Secretary of War for Air, 1946–1947; Secretary of the Air Force, 1947–1950; U.S. Senator (Dem.) from Missouri, 1953–.

THURMOND, STROM: b. 1902; Governor of South Carolina, 1947–1951; States' Rights candidate for President of U.S., 1948; U.S. Senator (Dem.; then Rep.) from South Carolina, 1954–.

WELKER, HERMAN: b. 1906, d. 1957; U.S. Senator (Rep.) from Idaho, 1951–1957.

WILLIAMS, G. MENNEN ("Soapy"): b. 1911; Governor of Michigan, 1949–1960; assistant Secretary of State for African Affairs, 1961–1966.

WILSON, CHARLES ERWIN: b. 1890, d. 1961; vice-president and president, General Motors Corporation, 1929–1953; U.S. Secretary of Defense, 1953–1961.